Emotioneering

BUSINESS RESULTS

— Melissa Curran

Dedicated to Daddy -

"You'll figure it out"

Hugh Mainwaring

1949 -2015

Emotioneering Business Results. Copyright © 2022 by Melissa Curran. All rights reserved.

FIRST EDITION

No portion of this book may be reproduced in any form without written permission from the publisher or author, except as permitted by U.K. copyright law except in the case of brief quotations embodied in critical articles and reviews.

Independent Publishing Network.

ISBN 978-1-80068-614-4

Contents

1. Introduction ... 1
   Welcome! Your Emotioneering Future Begins
     Why Me?
     What is Emotioneering?
     Why On Earth Does This Matter?
     Emotioneering in Business

2. People ... 21
   Where all Business Begins

Who Are You Looking For? ... 23

Are They Competent? ... 27

Who Are We? ... 31

Skillionaire ... 33

Where Do They Come From? ... 37

Shortlist or Selective List? ... 41

Choosing Your People ... 45

The Habit-Forming 90 ... 49

Saying Goodbye ... 55

3. Engagement   59
   High Performance is All About Discretionary Effort

Know Them   63

The Big Human Needs   67

The Driving Seat of Motivation   71

Always Believe In Your Goal   75

Rewards & Incentives   79

Gaining Buy-In   83

Analytics Tools & Software   87

Opportunities To Grow   91

Surveys & Feedback   95

Products & Prices   99

What's On Your Mind?   103

Accountability   107

4. Activities   111
   The Winning Combination

Analysis & Data   115

The Biggest Impact   119

The Morning Rally   121

The Power of The Town Hall   125

Training Your People   129

Observations   133

Coaching Your Team	137
Strategy Meetings	141
Team Meetings	145
Halfway Catchups	149
Namaste In The Game	153
Who Needs A Hero?	157
5. Culture The DNA of a Company	161
Vision	165
Mission Statement	169
Values	173
The Ministry of Fun	177
Let The Light In	181
Out Of The Workplace	185
The Number One Reason People Don't Open Up	187
Seeing is Believing	191
Ethics & Social Commitment	195
Standards of Excellence	199
Leadership	203
6. Execution It's In The Doing Not The Talking	213
Belief	217

Remove The Roadblocks	221
Ownership	223
Find The Who For You	225
Training Not A Magic Pill	227
Excellence Is Not Convenient	231
Actions & Follow Up	235
Accountability	237
The Narrative To The Numbers	241
Inspiring Action	245
7. Conclusion	249
Acknowledgments	255
Notes	261
About The Author	265

One

Introduction

♥

Welcome! Your Emotioneering Future Begins

Firstly, thank you for choosing this book to help you on your journey and congratulations on wanting to learn more. I am over the moon that you have decided to help yourself and your people. This book is for leaders in the service industry who are looking to have a competitive advantage, increased profits and highly engaged teams. Business Owners, Chief executive officers, chief operations officers, executive directors, HR directors, senior management or middle managers. If you have a team of people and want to have better performance then this is the book for you. It will provide you with many HR, operations and performance initiatives to implement with your team to Emotioneer Business Results.

You could also be experiencing something similar to some other people I know. Check them out -

Sally is a business owner who has been running her service based company for 10 years and has built it from the ground up. She is not sure how to get the best out of her people, they keep asking for pay rises although she knows there is no feedback being given to help them understand their performance. She knows time and knowledge are against her. Sally thinks "I wish I knew someone who could help with this."

Edward is a CEO who wants to work on more visionary projects although he is without a people and performance strategy to give him peace of mind that the business will continue while he is off launching a podcast or writing his book. He thinks 'why can't they run everything smoothly without conflict?'

Morgan is the founder of her automotive business for 12 years wants to scale her business although without the framework she needs there is no predictability to reach the goals she is looking for. She thinks 'if only someone had something for me to follow'.

Peter is the HR Director across two large retail locations. The board and stakeholders are wanting lower employee turnover and absence rates with an increase in profit. He knows the leadership team needs more support to provide performance management and the skills to do it. He doesn't have a performance or training manager to help him, he also doesn't know how to track the effectiveness of the project or know where to start. He thinks "If only I had more resources and an expert to ensure we get this right".

Jude is a people manager looking for a promotion in a call centre. When they had their review they were told to be more innovative, work on their leadership style and drive better results to get to the next level. Jude thinks "I don't feel I get the support or mentorship to know how to do this.".

What's great about this book is that whether you are like Sally, Edward, Morgan, Peter, Jude or any other type of leader in the service industry you can discover a way to really help you and your team move forward in 5 key sections packed with many practical strategies to gain the business results you are looking for. Covering people, engagement, activities, culture and execution.

Why Me?

I will never forget the famous quote that David Hughes said, 'Ambition is critical' and he was referring to the home town that I was brought up in. This is the quote that lines the walkway out of Swansea train station. From the perspective of other people, ambition can be seen as something to point a finger at and have a critical view of. I choose to look at it in a way that ambition is a critical part of your future. Dylan Thomas is also supposed to have said 'Swansea is the graveyard of ambition'. We do not know if he truly said this but many people from South Wales will recall being told it as they were growing up. Whether true or not, it certainly would not become reality for this young woman that was on a mission to make a difference from an early age.

"Ambition is critical" - David Hughes

We can only ever start to connect the dots when we look back. Born and raised in Swansea, South Wales, to Hugh and Sonia, I am grateful to be from a hardworking, loving and encouraging household. We didn't have the best of everything and I distinctly remember seeing a small amount of rust when riding around on the bike that had been given to me on my 7th birthday by my parents. Of course, it was second hand and I was reminded every day of how lucky and how grateful I should be to have shoes on my feet and a bed to sleep in at night, as many were not in such a position. This I believe, no matter where I go or what I do has kept me grounded. I was a whirlwind of enthusiasm, dancing, singing, chatting and always curious about the world asking many why questions which at the time I'm sure took my mum and dad to the edge of their patience once or twice. Ha!

My dad was an engineer and toolmaker by trade. He would always be tinkering with things, fixing things or making improvements, much to his delight when he had finished. Always proud to show us what he had done. As I grew up though, I found he was a great listener and I went to him often with things that were on my mind, although he NEVER gave me the answer, he would simply say "You'll figure it out". When it came to teaching though he had patience, teaching me to ride a bike and drive a car because he was passing on those skills. When it came to solving life problems though, he wanted me to at least attempt to solve them first. To which, I always did.

My mum was a singer and performer, always a lover of music at home. Stevie Wonder, Diana Ross, the Beatles, the Beegees and Barbara Streisand were often on the record / CD player. Mum encouraged me to try many things, tap dancing, singing, piano, theatre groups and once she realised I could do different accents sent me to elocution lessons to learn how to use my voice effectively. Her mantra was always 'let's go again' or 'one more time'. Practising constantly until her songs were right, which saw her working as a singer on cruise ships as we grew older. From both of these strong parental influences, I learned to love, look for solutions with an engineers mind and to express myself. I was also enthusiastically into sports, hockey, volleyball, running and athletics. My energy was relentless.

Sadly after my grandfather passed away my mum and dad got divorced, which I know was tough on both my parents, from losing a parent to then splitting up and having two young children was of course going to be hard. Fast forward through the years and when it came to college I had two clear distinct paths that were being considered. I was strong at Performing arts, Media, English, Sports and Science. So I was at a crossroads although settled on the path of Performing arts.

Before starting college I developed a skin disorder called Psoriasis, which seemed to come out of nowhere. It covered almost 90% of my body, the only place that it did not were my head, hands and feet. Being young and not knowing how to deal with this (when boys and hanging out with your friends were considered to be extremely important to a 16-year-old), I made the decision to hide it. It could be blazing summer heat and I would cover myself up from head to toe. Very few people knew. Until one day I had to perform in a show that used costumes that were extremely skin-baring. I felt sick and encouraged by my mum as well as the lecturer at the time to just do it anyway and not hide anymore, I reluctantly did. What followed was a world of sorrow. Friends stopped calling, I was excluded, left out and felt extremely alone. I get it, to other youngsters that didn't understand, I looked diseased. And so I was cast out, depressed and lonely. I decided that the performing arts world wasn't for me. At the time I thought it was because I thought it was a very judgemental industry, I now believe it was more because I didn't want to be seen anymore.

I was approaching 18 and coming from a now single home the cost of living and education meant that I had some tough decisions to make. I decided to get a full-time job, whilst pursuing sports science and performance on top of work knowing I would now be paying for every course that I chose to do from my own pocket. I was also referred to a specialist for my skin and within a year my body confidence started to come back even if my trust in other humans did not fully yet.

My first full-time job was selling advertising space for the local paper. I think the director saw the energy and communication skills I had as raw talent. So there I was barely 18, wearing a business suit, not really understanding what I was doing, turning up to bars and clubs to present ideas to businessmen as well as explaining the possible return on investment if they were to place an advert in the paper. This was when I really started to understand sales and marketing. I remember one of the owners of ICE Bar asking me 'how will I know it will work?'. So I quickly had an idea to suggest he make the advert a two for one voucher on all alcopops (remember them) with a valid until date, then he would see the number of people who brought them in. To my delight, I went back two weeks later to find him smiling from ear to ear, with a stack of our voucher adverts cut out and behind the bar. It worked! Over the next few years, I worked across many companies in call centres, car insurance, leisure centres, gyms, mobile, retail outlets, hospitality, food and beverage all whilst continuing my professional development to qualify for courses that were aligned with my purpose. It was not uncommon for me to have two jobs at the same time as well as studying. I had a passion for people and helping them. This is what made me great at service and sales, as well as being able to pass on the skills or things I learned to others.

I worked my way up to sales and performance management but I really decided that I wanted to be in the fitness industry so I moved to London. My first job there was working as an assistant fitness manager, for a local authority leisure centre, being told not to expect too much because people didn't really pay for personal training or seem to want it. I looked that challenge straight in the face and within 3 months had MANY personal training clients so much so that within another 6 months made the decision to set up my own personal training and sports massage business. After a few years as an entrepreneur, as busy as I was I started to suffer from my mindset, feeling lonely, not understanding the impact of networking or how to scale, plus I was in London. The looming rent payments every month scared the hell out of me. I decided to close up the business and returned to what I knew, sales and service, this time though in a vertical I had never covered before. I remember crying on the way back from the interview, not because I thought I wouldn't get it but because I thought I would. It felt like a big step back at the time. If only I knew what I know now.

I remember the sales managers face when he explained my target and then I replied with "what is the top person bringing in? Because that will be my target!", "Don't try and run before you can walk!" he said. Don't you just love it when someone tries to stifle ambition?! (ambition is critical remember). Much to the managements amazement within two months I was top of the leaderboard. I had the highest number of passengers and service scores that defined my integrity. I started to climb the ladder, much to the dislike of some of my peers that had been there for way longer. The toxic atmosphere this created and the workplace bullying that followed was intense. There were times that I just prayed the train wouldn't stop so that I didn't have to get off. Eventually, I had to do something about it and I want to thank the senior management at this point for being the leaders that did not stand for it or allow it to continue, as difficult as it was for me to express myself in those dark times. I had previously been bullied and excluded for the way I looked, now it was for my abilities and personality.

The head of operations at the time saw how interested I was in performance and knowing I was a strong coach started to show more of the data analysis plus performance management techniques that could be used. The results my team were able to achieve with these new insights and when I started to coach them were amazing! I soon was asked to coach other teams and take on people with more challenging behaviour, with the results being seen and my passion to help others I was also given the new starter academy to induct all the new employees. Soon I pioneered a training and development department with other quality analysts and coaches. Our goal, was to close the skills gaps whilst achieving record-breaking sales, with high quality and exceptional service scores. I loved it and was also asked to implement performance management for the sister company. I was now feeling so fulfilled, giving way more discretionary effort than I ever had, attending board meetings and really making a difference.

That was until April fools day many years ago. I had been called to a board meeting of 12 other directors and myself. It was a morning meeting and following some miscommunication or a cross of values, one person decided to verbally address me in a way that I can only describe in my opinion as, scary, unnecessary, embarrassing and intimidating. Their face turned red with anger. Something had triggered this reaction. Not one person said anything. Potentially, partly shocked and scared themselves. I stayed silent until the end of the meeting although I was fighting back the tears. I thought how could this leader, who I had given a lot of my blood, sweat and hard work speak to me like that in front of everyone. The carpet felt pulled from under me. I decided that I would hold my head high, complete my work for that day, and then write a letter of resignation never to return again.

I would never let my previous leaders, family or friends speak to me like that and think it was ok, I wasn't about to let them think it was either. The way I saw it was that if I was to stay this sent out a message to everybody else that this was okay and an acceptable way to treat people. I know that this was not their intention and I know that they were sorry although the mindset of just passing it off as just part of who they are was not something I could agree with.

We almost all have the potential and the ability to change our behaviour. We have since mended our relationship and I have a lot of respect for them, it was years ago and we have both grown as people. I too understand that no one sets out the 101 of relationships in the workplace when you are starting out. We only know what we know. I do know though that you and I do not have to accept this behaviour from the people who dish it out, April fools day or not. I am by no means the perfect leader and I have learned my lessons along the way and have shared many of them in chapters that follow.

Looking to the future, I was wondering what on earth the universe had in store for me now. I applied for many roles and I remember being extremely excited about the prospect of working as a performance management consultant for an American born global consultancy firm that supported the service industry, retail, leisure, hospitality, call centres and automotive were their verticals. Are you starting to connect the dots now? These were all industries that I had experience in. I was a business generalist although people operations and performance specialist. I had worked on the inside of a company being the manager understanding different departments and how to work across them and now I was the consultant from the outside in, looking to transform cultures, create highly engaged teams and results that the clients hadn't even dreamed of. It's a very different world though to harness the ability to influence change when no one reports to you and ultimately you are not the decider of the outcome, even though you are held accountable for the relationships and results.

I soon found that I was being given the more challenging accounts or being asked to visit clients that others believed there wasn't much more potential for and managed to turn them around. I then was offered a role to run the academy for new consultants joining the business to train them in performance consultancy as well as flying all over the world, mainly Europe, to drive performance management initiatives and support the wider team.

During the whirlwind of all this, my dad collapsed in front of me of a heart attack when I was visiting home over the weekend. He had suffered diabetes for years and there was no defibrillator close to our home so whilst we carried out CPR and could keep him alive long enough for my brother to say goodbye, we lost him within 24 hours. The trauma of that day was a lot and it started to manifest itself into a fear of flying, I suffered panic attacks constantly. Some people asked me why I took a job knowing I had to fly with this fear and panic. The simple reason was that I was not going to let that beat me. There were many people for me to help and I knew it was a case of mind over matter. There came a point though when my self-help measures were not working so I decided to get some talk therapy and CBT with a counsellor. This was a massive turning point for me. I worked through all the previous experiences I had, I became even more self-aware, reflective and managed to create a toolkit of ways to overcome the fear and the panic although now I was left with the sense of missing home. Not sleeping in my own bed half the time, not seeing my husband and not being able to walk my own dog. I developed a strategy to leave, which was an extremely difficult decision to make. I worked with some of the best people I have ever worked with. I knew deep down that I wanted to create my own people operations and performance consultancy. I had all the skills and was being sent like a silver bullet everywhere else so I thought why not?! The statement in itself though makes it sound easy. It has not been and I appreciate the journey that every business owner and entrepreneur has been on. Meanwhile, I had also decided to train as a counsellor to understand how to be able to listen to people the way I had been listened to and how to respond during those difficult conversations. Over the course of my life, I have continued to learn and complete courses alongside my work, for example, project management, coaching, HR management, digital marketing and many more. Ensuring that the key skills and theories are implemented in what I do. This almost brings us up to today and you reading this book.

I believe in creating a world where no one leaves a company due to poor leadership. They might leave due to wanting a new opportunity or because they decide to change their vocation. In my opinion, I just don't think it is acceptable for people to feel scared, bullied, humiliated, overlooked or like they don't belong because a leader isn't skilled enough or being held accountable for the relationships and results within their team. People deserve more, to feel fulfilled and have a sense of purpose for their work that will impact their whole life.

> "I believe in a world where no one leaves a company due to poor leadership!"

It's often not a leader's intention, they haven't been shown or educated in a different way. A better way. That will bring about much better results and a sense of fulfilment about their role. Helping others to grow and reach their potential.

> Let's align on these though -

> It's not okay for people to be spoken to badly especially in front of others

It's not okay for people to feel anxious or scared to speak up

It's not okay for people to not be recognised for great work

It's not okay for people to feel undervalued

It's not okay for people to feel isolated or that they do not belong

It's not okay for people to have the dread of returning to work after some time off

It's not okay for people to be bullied or harrassed

It's not okay for people to not be encouraged and supported

It's not okay because we can do something about it.

We deserve better. Your people deserve better. You can be better. We can be better.

I have -

Travelled the world to help teams have better performance, professionally develop their people, and have world-class engagement.

Delivered over 1,000 in-person workshops

Delivered over 15,000 hours of coaching (from frontline employees right up to the executive level)

Helped all my clients so far achieve record-breaking results

Used the word 'people' over 90 times
in a 45 minutes podcast as a guest

Spoken at many events for companies
such as Dell, Swoop Technologies,
Disability Conversations, JPI Media,
and many more.

Been a UK Radio Breakfast Show
presenter and crashed the website on
the first day

Hit the Top 50 UK Podcast Chart
with The Emotioneering Podcast and
ranked in the Top 2% globally out of
2.7 million shows, and listened to in
over 80 countries

Been awarded "Game Changer of the
Month" featured in Creative Talk
Magazine

I now play volleyball for a league team, paddleboard when the weather allows, spend time with my husband, friends, family and of course take our french bulldog off for a walk to the beach or the mountains. I am fuelled with the passion to help others to reach their potential and gain true fulfilment from seeing my clients succeed often getting results that they didn't believe possible. Hosting the Emotioneering Podcast has also given me the opportunity to learn from some of the best people in the service industry when interviewing them as my guests. Thank you all!

From working with my clients though I have found that the way that I do this is with a framework that I have been unknowingly using over the years to bring about these results. I have realised that there is a world of businesses and people out there that can benefit from this knowledge. They may be smaller SMEs that don't get the support from larger corporate performance consultants or they have hired people that they thought could do the job and they can't. There are 13 key areas of focus that make up this framework which I call the Emotioneering Business Blueprint. I use this to analyse a business and look at opportunities for people operations, learning and performance improvement.

What is Emotioneering?

Well, let's look first at what it is not. Tesla, an incredible brand, incredible company and fantastic mission. They are creating high-performance vehicles. They're continuing to improve and tweak or adapt their vehicles to improve their skill, their ability, and to enhance their performance all the time. They will continue to do that. They're driven by electricity. People are not driven by electricity or diesel or petrol. People are driven by emotion.

> "People are driven by emotion"

The brain's job is not to help us thrive, its job is to help us survive. This survival mechanism means that we have a negative bias to focus on the negative to help us survive. The thalamus is responsible for controlling how we react or respond to situations and this is where emotion is believed to come from. There are two routes that our brain creates emotions. The unconscious and the conscious routes. The unconscious is the quick and reactive route and the conscious is the slow and more considered route.

Let's discuss the unconscious route. The brain triggers the unconscious route within 6 seconds. For our survival, this is what will trigger the fight or flight response so the speed is critical. The thalamus triggers the unconscious assessment before the amygdala does a rapid assessment of the threat of a situation and sends info to the rest of the body which will then activate hormone release which is what determines our immediate reactions. Think about when someone jumps out at you, or you are jumping out on someone as a surprise and they scream, freeze in fear or run away, this is an example of the unconscious emotions that are formed. Now the challenging part here is that if there has been trauma or significant threat in the past, the amygdala remembers and will be automatically activated again in the future. Think about when I mentioned the panic attacks following my dad passing so suddenly.

The more slow and considered, conscious route to emotions, reactions and responses is route two. After the brain has run route one, the unconscious, it then scans the environment again slowly to create a more conscious response. The thalamus triggers a slow assessment this time. The sensory cortex uses stored memories and sensory information on the current situation to adjust emotional responses accordingly.

Reactive vs responsive. They are called 'first responders' at the scene of an accident for a reason and not 'first reactors'.

Almost every single one of us will have an unconscious route to our emotions. So our first reaction is an emotional one, not a slow and considered one.

We are emotioneering human performance, not engineering it! We help people to increase their ability and their skill. In order to do that we have to speak to their hearts. You have to connect with a person emotionally to do that. It's our brain's first instinct to act with emotions and this is based on our experiences in life. Emotioneering is about human performance. It's how we grow as individuals, as well as how we grow within the workplace. It's how we improve our relationships, how we improve our skills, and how we improve our abilities to have more fulfilled lives and careers.

> "We are emotioneering human performance, not engineering it!"

Why On Earth Does This Matter?

Well, for us as individuals, it can actually be argued that we have one overall motivation in life, to have meaningful relationships with people. That's the only way to fulfilment, some people will say. It's our relationships with loved ones, with friends, family or work colleagues. It's how we interact socially that is going to make us feel much happier and will prolong our life. This also applies to organisations or businesses, because we work with people and not robots. Although the robots are there much more, the majority of the time in a service-based industry we're working with people. It's knowing how to motivate and inspire those people. It's about giving meaning to what they do, which will equal the results, engagement and culture of your business.

Then how do we help people to build better relationships, lives and careers? It all starts with moving people from fear towards confidence. Being confident in knowing who they are and being empowered to express themselves. That starts with coaching and leadership. Many people say to me, "How do you have so much confidence?"

I can honestly say that I know the secret to confidence and that "Fear is a reaction courage is a decision" said Churchill and I'll add "Confidence is an outcome". The more we can help people believe in themselves to be more comfortable with making courageous decisions then they will start to change their lives. Confidence is then just an outcome of action and proven possibility over and over again. Once you've done something you realise It was never half as bad as your mind had simulated it to be and you can envisage doing it again even if at the time you felt nervous.

> "Fear is a reaction, courage is a decision and confidence is an outcome"

Here is the emotioneering triangle:

FEAR

CONFIDENCE   COURAGE

The Emotioneering Triangle
By Melissa Curran

Modern Mind Group

If you're a CEO out there now, and you want to have a legacy, your wish, your dream, your purpose and your strategy are all focusing on the legacy. It means that you're going to leave something lasting behind. Then it really has to be about the people because that culture or that education and the way that people feel about what they do, within the company, has to continue once you're gone. Yes, it's about your results although It's about the reactions as well. That starts by emotioneering with a modern mindset.

Emotioneering in Business

In business leaders don't always understand that their people are driven by emotion. Wanting to evolve, elevate, transform and change for the future will require understanding the Emotioneering Triangle to help people embrace change, to learn new skills and to feel fulfilled in their life. Emotioneering is connected to every process, every initiative, every piece of communication, every part of the brand identity, and every part of the business DNA.

Every time you change the commission structure

You are emotioneering!

Every time you give someone feedback

You are emotioneering!

Every time you implement new technology

You are emotioneering!

Every time you have a meeting

You are emotioneering!

Then you are left wondering about whether you should have said it that way, or done it that way, or could it have been better?

This is also emotioneering although internally for yourself

So I'm going to help you be better at it -

Imagine feeling satisfied with the performance of your team...

Imagine having peace of mind that the team can operate without you and you can sleep well at night...

Imagine a team that worked so well together that it felt like a dream...

Imagine having the predictability to be able to scale your business...

You can have that almost every day!

That day will be when you implement everything I am about to tell you.

Remember, I've told you, I've sat on each side of the fence, I've helped teams from within a business and I've consulted from the outside in with a fresh set of eyes. Everything I am about to tell you I have done and I know that you can do too.

I promise you that when you implement everything that I am about to share with you then you will increase profits, have highly engaged teams and record-breaking results.

Every minute wasted is another minute away from the results that I have told you are possible.

If you are ready to make a change then start today and you too can be on your way to emotioneering business results.

Go for it!

♥ · ♥ · ♥ · ♥ · ♥

Two

People

♥

Where all Business Begins

People. Where all business begins. I once sat opposite an executive director of a global organisation where they proceeded to tell me that, "Processes come first!", my response was, "People come first!", we couldn't be more different in our thinking. Poles apart. The most valuable resources in any business are the people. They come first and as far as I'm concerned always will.

£15,000 is what it costs on average when you are replacing or hiring a new employee. This refers to the total cost and time of the whole hiring process, not including their salary or equipment. Pre-hire and post. If a company replaces just 10 people that's £150,000. The amount can really add up.

Have a look at the people that are in the current team and ask yourself who is your favourite employee? Then ask yourself, why? Were they one of the first people to join the company? Do they make more money than everyone else? Do they get it? Do they give more discretionary effort than the rest of the team? Once you know why then ask yourself how were they recruited? Did they approach you? Did they apply for a job post?

Fill this in...

When I think of my team, the first person that comes to mind is _____.

Why? They are usually one of the founders and original members of your company! Their enthusiasm for work really does shine through in their performance daily. It's almost like they were destined to be working with you right?!

Who Are You Looking For?

♥

A few years back at a conference a friend called Rawiri, and I were having dinner and I asked him "If you were going to build an ALL-STAR WINNING team with the top 10 people you know or have worked with who would be in it?" Now, we also knew a lot of the same professionals and consultants, so the question kick-started a great discussion about why and what qualities or skills those people had that made them great for the team. There have been many times in my career where I have met people that are all-star players. That have the company values and DNA to the core, they make your customers feel great, they make the team feel great when they are around, and they hardly give you any challenges (Nancy, Casey, Alex, Driss, Halina, Sharon, Tony, Jacob, Ammar, Dora, Julie, Stephane, Danielle, Gintare, Filipe, Christine, Kelly, Tom, Neil, Sarah, Mark, Stephen, Luciano, Diogo, Tiago, Liliana, Alvaro, Vicky, Dimitri, Freddie, Manuel, Yasemin and Nuno this point is dedicated to you – superstars! Although there are many more along the journey that ROCK and you know who you are. Keep being amazing!). Think about your favourite places to go, the gym or maybe a restaurant. Who is that person that goes out of their way? Do they remember your name? Those are the all-stars. The question is how do you get more of them into your business?

Your People are the Real Difference

In a service-based industry, there is no getting away from it, almost every member of the team will have to face and talk to the customers. In a big world of choice, your people are the only real difference that a company can make. It's about how they make others feel. The team and the customers. The challenge can be in pinpointing those qualities that make these ALL-STAR team members. Plus, I believe and from what I have seen it is often about attitude above everything. Skills can be learned well with the right attitude. It is often harder to adapt someone's attitude and behaviours. So, let's focus on really knowing what qualities to look for.

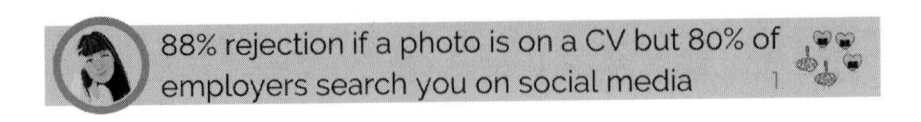

> 88% rejection if a photo is on a CV but 80% of employers search you on social media

Emotioneering It

Over my career and spending time being a worker in the service industry, as well as a consultant working with thousands of different people, I have developed an anagram to guide others to find the right person.

That anagram is GREET and it stands for -

Genuine

Recognition Driven

Enthusiastic

Empathetic

Team Player

You want someone who is able to GREET people in your service business. Your Team, your clients, your customers, and your partners.

1) Take these qualities and list all the people in your team. On a scale of 1 – 10 mark them against each quality. Are your most challenging members of the team lower on the scale when you complete it?

2) Use GREET as one of the benchmarks when interviewing people in the future especially if they are going to have to interact a lot with others. If the skills of the final candidates are the same choose the ones that rank higher on the GREET assessment scores.

· ♥ · ♥ · ♥ · ♥ · ♥ ·

Are They Competent?

♥

A great client I had the pleasure of working with for the service industry was having requests from team members for pay rises or changes to their benefits when, unfortunately, the feedback from the management team was that they believed the employees were not up to standard. My understanding was that the employees didn't really know what was expected of them. This was because the team were being recruited based on a set of tasks and experiences rather than clear behaviours or competencies. Following discussions with the team and detailing what was required of each role we managed to come up with a clear set of competencies that could be trained to and to be able to provide feedback based upon. These for example were time management and organisation, emotional intelligence, accuracy etc. What the senior management team also found out from that was that some of the team members exceeded expectations when it came to the competencies. This increased the whole team engagement and supported the performance goals for the business because when you focus on the behaviours and actions, the results will take care of themselves.

Behaviours Drive The Result

In a business, many often focus on the numbers and the tangibles more than the knowledge and behaviours that drive the result. This could be down to a lack of understanding from the leadership or the fact that the culture has been built this way. When we start to break down what it takes for high performance it is often a way of working through the process and applying effort or specific behaviours that drive the desired outcome. For example, I play Volleyball for Swansea, if I attempted to play every game without practice and without breaking down each component then applying the learnings, then that leaves a big opportunity for improvement. This would also cause BIG perceptions gaps that I will have in my own abilities. Leaving me to blame myself personally or start blaming others rather than appreciating what goes into building up to a level that produces results. Thankfully I have had Scott, Phil, Bart and Chris coaching our team as well as the support from my teammates. There is still so much more potential for everyone though.

What are Core Competencies?

These are the capabilities that comprise the strategic advantages of a business. They benefit the individual, the business and the customer. Core Competencies are defining characteristics,
behaviours and knowledge that help an individual or team to achieve results. Competencies and how well they are implemented and coached can make all the difference when developing a team that stands out from the competition and achieves world-class results.

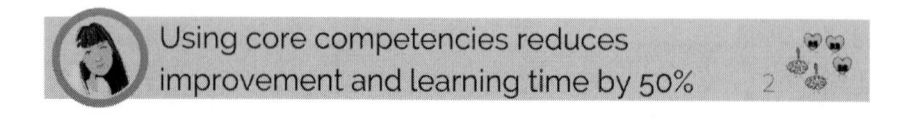

> Using core competencies reduces improvement and learning time by 50%   2

Emotioneering It

How They Work

Once the competencies are agreed upon they will fit across most, if not all, of the job roles within the business. The type of job role will determine the level of competency that is required for that position.

These could be graded on a scale of 1 - 5

1 = Unsatisfactory *(hardly anything on the description is met)*

2 = Improvement Needed

3 = Meets Expectations *(for their role)*

4 = Exceeds Expectations

5 = Exceptional (all the elements are met and more)

When recruiting the suggestion would be that you are aiming for a 3 or 4 out of 5 for the main competencies related to that role although would not expect a 5 (exceptional) this then allows for personal growth and development. This will also allow for succession planning.

For example:

Competency = Emotional Intelligence

- Maintains awareness of emotions and uses this to guide constructive thinking and actions.
- Takes ownership for their actions, understanding their strengths and weaknesses.
- Demonstrates self-control and recognises their own pressure points.
- Manages and is empathetic towards the emotions of others adapting their communication
- Delivers on commitments; admits mistakes.

Leadership Role Expectation = 4

Frontline Employee Expectation = 2

Explanation - The leader would be required to manage other people's emotions as well as their own. The frontline employee would not be expected to manage others' emotions yet and would not be directly responsible for others, although would be required to demonstrate a level of balance to their own emotions and may need support to understand their opportunities for improvement.

Core Competencies are recommended to be discussed in one-to-one sessions with team members regularly. These can help shape goal setting and performance reviews. As the business grows over the years and more roles or departments are added it is advised to improve, add, or change the competencies depending on the team and role requirements.

Who Are We?

♥

It was a rainy and extremely cold night in Vienna, at a work conference and we were off to have a walking tour of the city (No escaping the rain for this Welsh woman, hardly ever). Everyone was there from junior management consultants right up to the CEO. There I was, eager, humble, hungry, and driven. I turned to the COO I had been walking alongside and said, "So which personality type are you?", that afternoon we had been looking at the Myers Briggs 16 different personalities and had blocked them into 4 different groups. He smiled back at me and replied, "Great question Melissa, I have to be all of them!". I wanted to ask more questions but gradually and suddenly we were surrounded by a crowd as the walking tour had begun, so I was left to ponder on his response.

A Fixed Personality or Not

The challenge in a workplace is that there are going to be many different personalities or characters brought together to form teams and it's not likely that everyone will blend and work harmoniously. This could be through different values, beliefs, and cultural differences. It could also be different depending on how worldly-wise a person is from their life experience to that point. Let's call this cultural intelligence and emotional intelligence. What many of us want as leaders is for the team to trust each other, not to have anyone feel left out and to produce great results. Often a company will rely heavily on psychometric testing before the recruiting of candidates and based on the story above I am not convinced that this is an effective strategy for choosing those who will succeed in the role or team that you have.

Psychometric testing gives us an overview and a snapshot of the person's preferred method of thinking, chosen behaviours and communication style. For example, there is the Myers Briggs test and DISC profiling, although these do not, in my opinion, promote openly that as we grow as individuals our answers will also change. We have the ability to change through experience and much like the story above, I have seen over the years that my own answers to the profiling test have changed 3 -4 times. This has happened as I have evolved or was dependent on my environment, mindset, or role. It's important to understand that having the ability to adapt your style to your team is key to success.

> Reasons for losing customers or clients are 70% emotional intelligence related

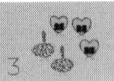

Emotioneering It

- Use psychometric tests as a guide and to encourage self-awareness not something to hold on to that cannot be changed.
- Instead, focus on the feeling that you get from the person in front of you and use the GREET model mentioned earlier. Hire based on attitude as well as skills and experience.
- Also, take one yourself and share it as well as ask your team too. This will help to understand different communication styles.
- If using the psychometric tests, then encourage them to be retaken to review the changes.

Skillionaire

♥

I have always been a 'why' learner turned 'how' learner. What I mean by that is that if there was a big enough reason or purpose and it was going to help me in my mission then I would figure it out and learn the 'how'. I believe this influence came from my dad who was an engineer. It didn't really matter what I faced in life, whatever challenge I had. He would listen and say, "You'll figure it out!". It wasn't until after he passed that I realised he NEVER gave me the answers. His engineer's mind wanted me to learn and try. My mum's influence through performing arts meant that repetition was a constant thing and that's how you got better, by rehearsing. So, take this combination and I became very open to trying, even if it failed and have the tenacity to continue to work at it until I found the solution. I believe this serves me very well in the people operations and performance industry.

The reason I say this is that anything, absolutely anything can be learned. If you haven't read it, I highly suggest reading the book Grit: The Power of Passion and Perseverance by Angela Duckworth in there she details the formula for Achievement which is, Talent X Effort = Skill, then Skill x Effort = Achievement. Boom! This is genius. She goes on to state the proof that hard work beats talent when talent refuses to work. If you've got the time and resources, then definitely upskill your team otherwise it's the choice of hiring skilled employees from outside and then that will also cost more in time and resources.

We talked about competencies a little earlier. Skills underpin competencies, as well as knowledge, attitude, and habits (or as I referred to earlier, behaviours.) Competencies are the umbrella over all the others. For example, just because I have learned to pass a volleyball and have done it many times (skill) the questions would be, how much do I practically apply it in my life? Is it too fast or too slow? (Habit) Do I know how and why it is done that way? (knowledge), do I do it calmly or with anger? (attitude). These combined then will equal a level of competence.

Doing What They've Always Done

The challenge for a business, based on this skills subject, can often be to keep up with the skills that are required in today's environment. People may have been hired based on attitude and now companies require their employees to become skilled at doing a new certain task. These skills can be human skills for interacting or technical skills. For example, being skilled to adapt questions for different customers vs being able to create a content post via graphic design software. Identifying these skills gaps in your organisation and supporting the people to grow their abilities is crucial to the future success of the business and results. There are so many ways a person can become skilled, but it is only through the practical application of the knowledge learned in training or the classroom that this can happen. It is also important to realise that as people stay with a company just because they have done a job for 10 years are they highly skilled at it? For example, have they improved and refreshed their skills or repeated the first year 10 times? Have they got better at what they do? Or stayed at the skill level they came in with.

> 36% of employees believe there is a mismatch between their skills and what are needed 4

Emotioneering It

- Look at each role in the business and decide what skills are required for each by doing a skills audit.
- Separate the human skills and the technical skills
- Then look at whether there are skilled people in the organisation that can train people on this skill or that can be used as a subject matter expert to create a training course
- For ones that cannot be obtained within the company look for accredited courses or experts of their craft to deliver the training so that the skill level of your employees can increase.
- Have a look at your job description for an entry-level employee and assess the skills and expertise you are asking for. Does it align with the pay grade and level of the role? For example, alarms bells would ring for me if a job description said something like 'Junior sales consultant, must have 3 years experience in using CRM systems.

Where Do They Come From?

♥

"I just go out and find them," said Laurence. He was an area manager that was not waiting for job posts and applications to land on his lap, he took the approach of actively and constantly being on the lookout for great service and salespeople for his frontline. At the local coffee shops, retail stores, hotels and restaurants. He would be armed with his business card and offer conversations about exciting job opportunities. After telling the person that they had impressed him and paying them compliments he hoped to actively recruit them or at least start a relationship for future opportunities that could come up. This of course is one active way of recruiting the right type of people. Now that you understand the GREET model, you will start to identify these ALL-STAR people everywhere. There are always two pools of people to recruit from. The internal pool could include contractors, temp staff, current staff up for promotion or team members looking for a change. The external pool is more competitive, from job boards to universities or headhunting through other companies, the question is how resourceful and proactive can you be? It really does matter where you source your people from.

Not Enough Flex

The challenge when it comes to recruiting the right people is that -

1) The internal pool of people you may not believe is ready or right for opportunities that arise.

2) The external labour market is another matter.

The competitive nature could all depend on the labour skill set and what has been chosen at college or university education. The competition that colleges also bring, so that maybe not as many choices on job vocations such as NVQs in the UK as an example. The world of choice that has now been created due to remote working being more on offer lowering restrictions to a global marketplace, competition on salary or even more so now the younger generation are wanting to align with the values of a company, asking questions about the purpose and sustainability as an example. It's not always about casting the rod and seeing which fish bites. Another challenge can be employer rating sites such as Glassdoor which could be tarnishing your reputation depending on leadership and the way things have previously been handled in the business.

Could you also be in a position where a role has been open for so long to external candidates that now someone internal has been doing an excellent job for 6 months and is then overlooked?

The last point is that the process internally may be too slow for the operations and growth needs of the business. Yes, HR does have to be involved although can the process be less restrictive and understood by everyone in the senior management team.

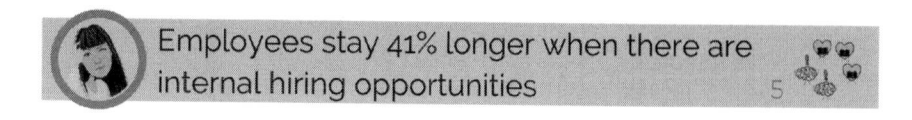

> **Employees stay 41% longer when there are internal hiring opportunities** 5

Emotioneering it

First, it is important to understand the corporate strategy for a flexible organisation – having a wide pool of internal and external workers to offer opportunities to is key to success because depending on demand and seasonality you can be very numerically flexible and financially flexible. There are two main pools to choose from to support your people needs and they fall into internal and external.

1. **Internal recruitment market** – current employees and people who already have a strong connection with the organisation such as former employees, temporary workers, sub-contractors and freelance workers
2. **External recruitment market** – people who have no previous employment history with the organisation, either because they have never before shown any interest in being employed by you, or they have unsuccessfully applied for a position before and their details have been retained on file for possible future use (this must be in line with GDPR and the Data Protection Act). It could also be about the relationships you have with recruitment agencies that will search for you.

Initiatives for The Internal Recruitment Market – Internal Job boards, management feedback from performance reviews and discussions with their team. Job swaps for people to learn about other departments. Emails, phone calls or conversations with temp staff, contractors, or sub-contractors.

Initiatives for The External Recruitment Market – External job boards online including government sites such as the job centre. Approaching service people that you meet that WOW you with their talents and abilities as I mentioned in the story previously. Social Media (over 80% of companies get passive recruitment this way). Open days at job fairs, schools, or universities. Signs up within the physical office if you have somewhere the public may see. Word of mouth; let people know about it in your social circle. Encourage the team to do the same, good people often know good people. Run an employee referral scheme.

Keep your relationships strong.

Shortlist or Selective List?

♥

"I quickly realised after 4 weeks of being over here and sending out my CV with my native name on it that I needed to change it to something that sounded more English, for the recruiters, for customers and my potential new teammates". This was a conversation I had with a close friend of mine in 2020 and they were telling me about their experiences regarding diversity and inclusion in the workplace. Knowing I never had to even contemplate this about myself really saddened and frustrated me. Why should anyone have to change their name to be able to get a job due to prejudice and biases that have been in the workplace for many generations? (To everyone that has ever had to, this one's for you).

I also recently was asked to host and facilitate at a Disability Summit organised by Sophia Nicholls and her incredible team on topics such as disability in relationships as well as disability in the workplace. What I found out was that remote and flexible working had been denied for many disabled workers prior to 2020 although when it was a must for all, it has now become acceptable. Whilst looking for the key individuals and ALL-STARS for our team let's understand that these come from many backgrounds, many abilities and ask ourselves are we (as companies) making the process fair for all? Do you address biases when we see them arise?

Unconscious Bias

We all have it and the more we can bring it to our consciousness, the better our decisions will be in creating a diverse, inclusive team and workplace. If you don't agree read Malcolm Gladwell's book called Blink and this will be eye-opening.

I've stood next to leaders that thin-sliced through the recruitment process based on gender, ethnicity or a name that is too challenging to pronounce. Let's just say there is a reason I don't stand next to them anymore. Let's not stand for unfairness when it comes to opportunity. Everyone deserves a fair shot and that's all people want. Often the recruitment process has been given to middle managers that are not as experienced and the senior leaders don't even realise this is happening and then wonder why the whole team is not diverse enough. I suggest that if this is you then "inspect what you expect" do a recruitment drive together and see the process and the way your leader's work.

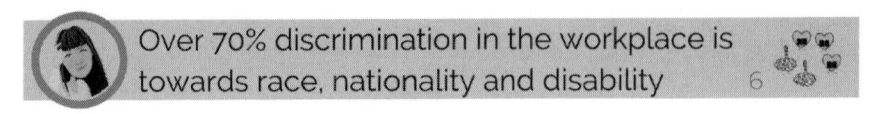

> Over 70% discrimination in the workplace is towards race, nationality and disability [6]

Emotioneering it

- If you are the leader of other managers spend time with them on the shortlisting process to understand their thought processes or ask your HR department. There is nothing quite like understanding it for yourself and having an opportunity to provide feedback.
- Look at your processes for recruitment and see how fair they are for people that apply.
- Continue to educate the team and facilitate discussions on conscious and unconscious bias that still exists.

Choosing Your People

♥

Whilst I've supported many businesses with their recruitment and interview process, I've recently had to go through this for myself (Thanks, Lauren Lepley-Caldon for encouraging me). As part of the UK Government Kickstarter Scheme, there was an opportunity to employ a young person under 24 that was unemployed. So, I set up the advert, worked with the job centre to organise a selection day that would have many people booked in for a 30 min slot with me to discuss the role and join the team. The things that were told to me prior to that day and throughout the process were all around not getting my hopes too high, not expecting too much and understanding that these people were not skilled at all.

I remained open and optimistic and when the time came, I was blown away. The challenge is that being a strong people leader you see the potential in everyone. These candidates came in and wowed me to the point that if I could have taken everyone I would have, this left me feeling quite emotional by the end of the day, so I decided to sleep on my decision. I could only take one person and whilst it probably made business sense to just pick the person with the strongest skill set and prior experience something told me to focus on the person who had the raw potential, and this opportunity would make the biggest impact for. So, I did that. My heart and head were aligned.

Up until now, I can say that I have not regretted my decision and they continue to wow me every week. Regarding the others, I thought long and hard about my own journey with recruitment and how annoyed it felt to just being told you were unsuccessful with no feedback to take forward, so I made sure that each person was told of the positives and the areas of opportunity. Interviewing people is not just a task list or a rational process, we are emotioneering the interview process. You really have the impact to make a difference in someone's entire life.

Space or Place

In a business, the recruitment and interview process can present many challenges. As I mentioned. Then you have to rely on the competence of your senior managers to effectively interview people and have the emotional intelligence to be aware of their ego or negative bias. Selecting the right candidates is also about striking the right balance between urgency and desperation. Your candidates will feel desperation a mile away. You may also make quick decisions that can cost you in the long run.

I was talking to a friend who is a business consultant recently who was supporting a client on the recruitment process and the hiring manager they were working with was ready to make an offer to the candidate and she asked one simple question to this hiring manager, 'If it was your money would you hire them?' and after a long pause the answer was 'No!'. The search continues. Also, consider how long or complicated the process is in relation to stages. If it is a quick process the wrong decisions could be made and it could send off the wrong signals to the candidate, if it is too long, they may lose interest.

27% of companies say that the cost of hiring the wrong person is over 50K

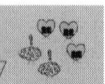

Emotioneering It

- Ensure a minimum of 3 stages – Screening Call, in-person/video interview and a final stage by someone more senior in the company or a 2nd opinion by a trusted advisor if you are a small business.

- Interview your top performers to refer to best practice expectations so that decisions are based on that and not the candidate you last saw.

- Remember – It's better to have the space, than the wrong person in the place.

- How much is their seat worth? – Workout how much their seat is worth in total to the company, not just the basic salary.

- Transparency / Full disclosure – Provide a clear view of the company and the expectations for the role. There is no point glamorising something when in reality they will come into the company and realise instantly that 'the video does not match the subtitles'.

The Habit-Forming 90

♥

On my exploration of happiness and fulfilment when creating our Emotional Intelligence training course, I found a great TED talk by Dan Gilbert on the Surprising Science of Happiness. His work and that of his team really researched what happened over 90 days from a life event. Due to the prefrontal cortex, human beings use it as an experience simulator. We try things out in our minds based on our experiences before we actually do it for real. Take for example "leather infused crisps with hints of skin from a back scratch" your brain probably put it through the simulator and decided it was disgusting (or there might be one of you that would be willing to give them a go, forcing yourself like in a bushtucker trial – go you! Unfortunately for you, these crisps do not exist).

Part of this means that employees will make up their own simulated experience based on what they think the start of their new job may be like. These expectations and interpretations happen on both sides. For the employee and the hiring manager. Often due to our impact bias, we can feel worse than something actually is in reality. Research has found that regardless of what happens to us in life after 90 days whether it was good or bad, it has no impact on our happiness and fulfilment and we start to habitualise to that routine. So, the 90–day induction period is important for expectations and simulations to be managed in a way that the new employee stays with the company for this period of time and are introduced to their role in a way that does not overwhelm them. Ever had anyone leave within the first week or first day and wondered why? Making it past the 90-day point is crucial to longevity for the business and the employee. The 90-day induction is the readjustment phase.

I recently employed a person for social media and content that I knew had not done any of this before. Whilst there were expectations of tasks in the job description, I chose not to train the employee on all of them straightaway. For the first 8 weeks, we focused on ensuring that the main priorities were trained to, and then new skills were introduced weeks 8 – 12. This allowed for feedback to be given and for them to feel competent in spinning a few plates before adding more. Of course, if they had been a more skilled or experienced person that was coming in this would be moved at scale although I would still not expect every task to be mastered straight away.

The Lasting Impression

The time that it takes to train and induct someone through a proper onboarding process is often underestimated and not always seen as important. The challenge with starting a new person in a business is, who should train them, when and on what.

The employee induction process is important to ensure that the employee transitions smoothly and efficiently into their role. Companies that have a well-planned employee induction process are likely to see lower levels of staff turnover as well as having more engaged employees. It can be a daunting experience for a new person to start to integrate into a new team, so it helps to take the start of their employment step by step to ease them into it.

You might very well hear people say, 'the burden of knowledge' or it could be referred to as 'the curse of knowledge'. Due to a human's cognitive bias, we can often assume that someone has the same background or base knowledge as us when in fact they don't. This means they could miss out on valuable information to be able to do their job correctly or to make great decisions. As a performance consultant over the years, I have delivered many training sessions, from frontline employees right up to the executive level. There have often been times that I have had to quickly adapt to the questions and audience knowledge level, to know when to stay longer on a subject or to scrap certain content which will not make sense. This was because what the client thought the team knew versus what they actually did know, were two different things. Many learning professionals and trainers know that this is something that cannot be avoided altogether because it is also a skill of facilitation to be able to adapt and make it meaningful to the learner. We cannot expect our teams to know everything, listen, assess and then deliver the right level for that person.

There are three barriers to learning that are, relational trust, perceptions gaps and capacity overload. I will go into more detail later in the book. The one I want to home in on here is capacity overload. The challenge can be as a leader, that if a person is contracted to 40 hours a week minus breaks that we want to fill every single minute with tasks for the job this can lead to capacity overload which is a big barrier to learning and often the desire to want to.

So, when inducting a new employee, have a look and see if there is any white space and if they have time to process the new information so that the knowledge is retained. Think about those times that the best ideas come to us, or we really take on new information. It is often when we have space in our lives and allows balance for different activities. When we can just be a 'human being' rather than a 'human doing'.

Employee exits cost 16% - 213% of their salary 8

Emotioneering It

An employee induction involves different roles and responsibilities, often HR management or the L&D team maintains responsibility for the planning and coordination of the activities as well as communication of the plan with the new employee. In a small business, this may be the owner or another senior member of the team.

Here are some of the things to consider when planning it

- Belief – Stories / Social Proof – share the success stories. Interview champions or brand ambassadors from within the company to share the message.
- Learning Centres – Whether you have a learning management system for eLearning solutions or an intranet where all of your processes and procedures live, these can be extremely advantageous to a new person eager to learn about the company and know where they can go for information.
- Best Practice – Can the best practice be clearly defined for their role? 'This vs That' or is there someone that they can spend time with that is the best in class example for what they will be doing.
For example, if you have hired a manager that will start in an underperforming store, then sending them to shadow and train in the top-performing store that you have will give them something to aspire to and see that it is possible. For frontline roles, this could be shadowing the best barista or the best call centre agent that you have. Let them see and experience the best of the best, the cream of the crop.
- Ask how they are / check-in with them – check the pulse on their involvement and how they feel about the start so far.
- White space - Analyse the schedule, does it include time for reflection and space in the agenda for thought?
- Everyone has a part to play –

Line Manager - A recommendation is for the line manager to have full accountability for ensuring the employee's full integration to the role as well as to monitor progress through the plan and provide as much support as possible.

Senior management - welcoming the new employees potentially with an informal chat as well as ensuring that the finance and resource for a proper induction plan are viewed as a crucial part of the business strategy.

Health and safety officer or manager - can ensure that the new employee understands any immediate risks or correct procedures for their safety.

Trade Union (if in place) - a representative could have time set aside to discuss the options available for the new employee.

Buddy or Mentor - Many organisations see the value in providing a 'buddy' or 'mentor' system at the start of a new team member starting so that they can help them to socialise and understand some of the team culture this is because workplace relationships have a large part to play in the success of the individuals as well as the organisation.

Finally, the full participation of the new employee in the induction process is vitally important as well as their behaviour during this process as this is part of their probation period. Having all levels participate in the induction process also provides different points of feedback for HR management as well as the line manager during this crucial time.

Line Manager - A recommendation is for the line manager to have full accountability for ensuring the employee's full integration to the role as well as to monitor progress through the plan and provide as much support as possible.

Senior management - welcoming the new employees potentially with an informal chat as well as ensuring that the finance and resource for a proper induction plan are viewed as a crucial part of the business strategy.

Health and safety officer or manager - can ensure that the new employee understands any immediate risks or correct procedures for their safety.

Trade Union (if in place) - a representative could have time set aside to discuss the options available for the new employee.

Buddy or Mentor - Many organisations see the value in providing a 'buddy' or 'mentor' system at the start of a new team member starting so that they can help them to socialise and understand some of the team culture this is because workplace relationships have a large part to play in the success of the individuals as well as the organisation.

Finally, the full participation of the new employee in the induction process is vitally important as well as their behaviour during this process as this is part of their probation period. Having all levels participate in the induction process also provides different points of feedback for HR management as well as the line manager during this crucial time.

Saying Goodbye

♥

I've worked in many contact centres in my time as a leader. Imagine the scene, an employee was marched out of the building, and everyone else was shocked that day. They had joined my team and we had a great relationship at first. We worked in a call centre and if anyone has worked in one you will know how performance-focused and KPI driven they are. Policies and procedures to follow with limited time away from your desk or the people that need to be served over the telephone. The factories of the phone world. This was an industry that I had had many years of experience in. The challenge was that this person was starting to take liberties away from the work to which the senior leadership team were coming down hard on me to address them and make it fair on the other members of the team.

Let's fast forward. It led to them sending an email threatening me. This of course was gross misconduct. This behaviour towards any member of staff would not be tolerated so they were dismissed from the company. It was quite an experience for me, as a young leader and I really liked them as a person and didn't realise the full extent of the consequences that would follow. Our behaviours really can impact our journey. What happened a year later was that I received a message from them apologising for the behaviour, to thank me for not allowing anyone to treat me that way and for the life lesson that had helped them to move forward. I think it's worth mentioning that letting someone go and addressing what is happening is an opportunity for a better environment for the people that stay as well as allowing them to find their true purpose and hopefully learn from the situation.

Here's another perspective -

"They just need to go! They are a nightmare to work with and I don't like them" this is a phrase that has often been said by people I have had to work alongside. Often this was the first thing that would come out of their mouth when it came to managers on-site visits or team members that didn't meet their expectations. It's not uncommon to hear this. What they are really saying in my opinion is – 'I haven't got the skillset or tools to figure out a way to work with this person or empower them to improve so they just need to go.' This happens far too often in the workplace. We can't expect to connect with everyone on a deep level although to come from an empathetic and compassionate standpoint says let me try and understand their circumstances, reserve judgement, and try and figure out what we can do to support them. Human behaviour is learned through our experiences in life, someone that is nervous could require reassurance to support their self-esteem, someone who appears angry could be really unhappy and unfulfilled in their life.

It's all about perspective and unless we ask questions then we really are just dismissing potential and casting judgement. Now I'm not saying that there isn't ever a time for dismissal or to fire someone, what I am saying is that have we had a second opinion? Have we considered all the options? Have we taken the time to adapt our style to the person's needs or supported them in all ways possible before making the final decision? I once had a conversation with an executive leader at an organisation who suggested asking two questions. First, if I had to hire them again tomorrow, would I? And the second, if yes is there somewhere else in the business that they would be able to excel?

The Hard Goodbye

The person that has now become a problem in the organisation often didn't start off this way. When they joined, they were full of enthusiasm and a desire to do well. Ask yourself what has the company done or what has changed in their life that has got them to this point? We often leave it much longer to fire someone than we need to or often want to. The challenge is it also starts to affect the rest of the team. Many employees want fairness when it comes to their work and if they see someone being treated differently or bending the rules, creating chaos, and then getting away with it then they can start to also feel like they don't belong before starting to look for another team. Do you want to lose your all-star players as well as the underperformers? There can also be an emotioneering challenge from the perspective that the leader may not know how to deliver feedback with candour to the employee and therefore shy away from it.

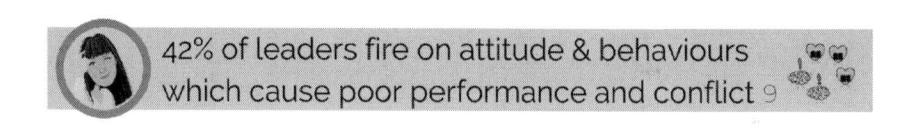

> 42% of leaders fire on attitude & behaviours which cause poor performance and conflict 9

Emotioneering It

- Ensure that you have given the person feedback, support, and the opportunity to improve. That is documented. Ask yourself, 'have I tried almost everything in my power and skillset?' Then, 'do I need to get help from someone else on this?'

- Ask yourself if I had to employ this person again tomorrow knowing what I know now would I? If the answer is 'YES' see if there is another suitable role for them. If the answer is 'No' then continue with the performance strategy for the individual.

- Ensure that they know the truth as to why it has come to a point where both parties cannot move forward.

- If you can give them advance notice support them to look for other work.
- If your first thought is to get rid of someone because of their behaviour then imagine that you can never fire them or hold them accountable with a formal disciplinary process, what would you do differently?

Three

Engagement

♥

High Performance is All About Discretionary Effort

Employee engagement is the degree to which a person feels mentally and emotionally connected to their work, the team and the organisation. So in business, we are building a society of hearts and minds combined.

Getting your employees to fully engage with their work is essential for any business. However, only world-class businesses achieve this at a high level.

Employee engagement can make or break a business because those who are engaged tend to have better performance than those that aren't. This becomes even more important when you consider how much discretionary effort, they're willing to put in, which directly impacts the revenue generation capabilities. Learning about these things from people within your company may bring great results but taking a look outside of the company might give greater insights which could help them improve faster compared to others. To create a high-performing team, it's important to understand the employees who work for you. Those relationships. Giving them the opportunity to share their thoughts or give input. It isn't necessarily about happiness, satisfaction or wellbeing, these are more to do with culture, it's about connection to the work.

Now it's not as clear cut as that, because culture is everything that we do so some initiatives spill over into employee engagement and will have a large impact. Many people ask if motivation and engagement are the same things... Engagement goes way beyond motivation.

Imagine you divided your team into 4 groups - Highly engaged, moderately engaged, barely engaged and actively disengaged.

Highly Engaged - These are your champions who tend to stay long term, they bring ideas to the table, helps other see the purpose of the company mission

Moderately Engaged - These are your strong workers although there seems to be something always holding them back

Barely Engaged - These are your people who behave indifferently and could be at risk of leaving

Actively Disengaged - This group are negative, disruptive to the rest of the team and have little or no desire to help the mission move forward

Now, I do want to add this though, any team member can move between each of the groups at any time. Of course, take a mental snapshot of it now although the goal is to move as many of the team to highly engaged and then keep them there. An actively disengaged, or barely engaged employee didn't originally start there. Something has happened over the course of their journey which is either internal to the company or external to their life. The question is can you get them back on the bus and equal opportunity to do so? I have seen it happen and I've been part of helping those transformations, so now I'm going to share my insights with you on what you can do to get there.

EMOTIONEERING BUSINESS RESULTS

Know Them

♥

We were the best team in the call centre and one of the team stood there shaking while the business manager and I waited to see what they had called a meeting for. I could see that he was extremely nervous. I started to feel nervous too and then he came out with it "I want to move team..." My ego took a dent and my first thought (because this is what the ego does) was to tell him to pack up his stuff and go if that's how he felt. After taking a moment to pause and listen more to what he was saying I realised it was my fault. I knew nothing about this person that was in my team, they had been made to feel so uncomfortable that they now wanted to chance their hand at another team before probably leaving the company altogether.

I asked them if we could both sleep on it and come back to discuss it in the morning. When we did, I apologised and took full responsibility. It was my fault that these employees did not feel like they belonged to the team, and I had not taken any time to get to know them. I asked them to give me two weeks to make more of an effort and if they still wanted to switch after that then I would understand. I started to pay more attention, spend time outside of work to understand their life and found they organised open mic nights and wrote poetic rap. Thankfully this amazing human stayed on the team. It's a lesson I will never forget.

It is Always Personal

The old mentality in the workplace is that it is wrong to get personal with your team. This is the most understood and underrated area of being a leader. If you don't want to get personal, then don't be a people leader. Relationships with your team and how you use your people skills are everything.

"People don't care how much you know, until they know how much you care" John C Maxwell.

It's the oldest and most effective strategy around.

C.A.R.E.

When it comes to leading teams often, we gravitate and connect with those that are easier to communicate with or those that are like us. The challenge is that a leader's job is not to be liked, a leaders job is to be absolutely LOVED. If you don't know your team they won't buy into you or want to be coached by you because to them they will be thinking 'what's in it for me?', 'they don't care about me'. or 'they are only doing this because they have to not because they want to'.

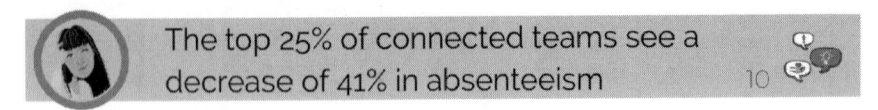

> The top 25% of connected teams see a decrease of 41% in absenteeism 10

Emotioneering It

- Get a piece of paper or mentally start to list the people in your team. Once you have finished, look at the bottom 25% of the list. Start there. Your brain has just told you who you like to spend time with the most by listing them in priority order subconsciously.

- Now take that list and start to ask yourself these questions – do they have a partner? If so what's their name? What is their birth month? Do they have a pet? If so what pet? What are their favourite hobbies?

What motivates them? What is their favourite food? What music do they listen to? – Now how full is the information? Have you been able to complete it?

- Spend time with every person in your team on a one-to-one basis with no agenda other than to understand their world. This person has hopes and dreams as well as a whole world outside of their workplace.

♥ ♥ ♥ ♥ ♥

The Big Human Needs

As mentioned in the last section the 4 big human needs have a big impact on how engaged an employee is in their role and how connected they are to the company. To recap they are, to be in control, to feel safe, to be valued and to belong. Let's take a sense of belonging and look at it in more detail.

Gallup has been studying employee engagement surveys for many years and one of the main factors to determine whether an employee was likely to stay and feel happy was the question 'do you have a best friend at work?'. I'm sure a lot of people pre-pandemic (before 2020) would say that they did.

These relationships are often built through bonding experiences, conferences, team outings, projects, teams, or classroom training as a few examples. In the new remote or hybrid workplace, this is a big challenge because many teams have reshuffled, the dynamics have changed, they are less likely to interact with each other face to face and through our work, at The Modern Mind Group, I am now starting to see more people answering 'no' to the 'do you have a best friend at work?' question. Therefore, this can directly impact engagement and loyalty to the business or team.

The Needy Workplace

To Feel in Control – There is a lot in the business world and in our roles that we are not in control of. People that have autonomy of how they schedule their day or do the projects often feel the most in control. When there is no autonomy at all, people are told what to do and when, without any flexibility, then this is where they can feel unfulfilled because it goes against their basic human needs.

To Belong – In teams (even in the playground growing up) there can often be ignorance, exclusion, bullying, clashes of personality that lead to conflict or loneliness. The biggest challenge can arise when this is accepted, dismissed, and not addressed by leadership. People want an inclusive work environment partly because of our internal need to feel accepted and part of a community. The ability to build relationships well and foster team spirit in many organisations is still a big opportunity.

To Feel Valued – Not being included in decision-making processes, finding out decisions after the fact, not receiving positive feedback or appreciation can make a person feel like they are part of the furniture and taken for granted. Often this isn't on purpose as it can even be the team members that you think highly of and would never want to lose, it's often because the service industry can also be extremely challenging, fighting fire after fire or because we aren't comfortable showing appreciation because we don't know the appropriate way to say something.

To Be Safe – Lack of trust, backstabbing and threatening behaviour can all be part of a fear-based toxic organisation. This can lead an employee to not want to open up to anyone, second guess their decisions and always be looking over their shoulder. There is also a physical safety aspect, having to work on a project without appropriate safety equipment especially in somewhere like the construction world, or a lack of regard for the environment that workers are in regarding temperature or physical hazards. Reports of harassment or inappropriate behaviour that have been overlooked. These can all lead to an employee feeling unsafe in the workplace. I'm sure they will want to run a mile away.

77% of companies are working on employee experience, which shows it is a big challenge, let's make sure there are effective changes put in place.

> 77% of companies focus on employee experience

Emotioneering It

- Understand what the four human needs are and live by them
- Ask yourself with each team or situation how it may affect each human need
- Ask yourself how many of these human needs are satisfied for you at the moment
- Look at the communication style of the leaders in the company and see if how they are communicating are in line with the 4 human needs

The Driving Seat of Motivation

♥

Steph was quite annoyed when I turned up to coach her at an airport car rental site. Not by my presence but by her life situation at the time. It was the 4th time her car had broken down this month. We started to discuss what was happening in her life. I asked her "What's your dream car?", to which she told me a white Audi, I then asked her if she had even looked into how much they cost, which she said she had not, so we checked it out together. Then we divided the cost over 12 months and worked how much commission it would take to get her dream car. Steph was a great service and salesperson. Delivering high results and I would class her as a top performer. Although she had never looked at setting such a personal goal for herself and connecting it with her targets as they had always been quite number orientated or based on the league table.

After we worked out that she could get the car that she had always wanted and how long it would take to get there I could see the sparkle and energy all over her face. What happened next was quite extraordinary. I went back to do a location visit and Steph was there, she jumped up and down and said, "Come and see this..." (can you guess what she wanted to show me?). There it was. The white Audi car that she had always wanted.

The best bit? It was only 16 WEEKS later not MONTHS! That is true engagement, Steph applied discretionary effort because the company goals were now very much aligned with her personal ones. I was over the moon for her. Ask yourself what do your team really want? Can you answer it for every team member?

Everyone's Favourite Radio Station

In the workplace, our communication regarding what is required for objectives can often be about what's in it for the company which is great when someone has become highly engaged already although combine that with their individual motivations and why it makes a difference to them, and you will see much higher levels of commitment to take action.

With so many different departments and priorities fighting for our attention as leaders if we don't know an individual's motivational drivers or make the effort to check in it can lead us to think or guess that it is money or just doing a good job when in fact it can be much deeper than what is on the surface. Making the time to find out can be a challenge although one that is absolutely worth it. WII FM – Everyone's favourite radio station which stands for – What's In It For Me?

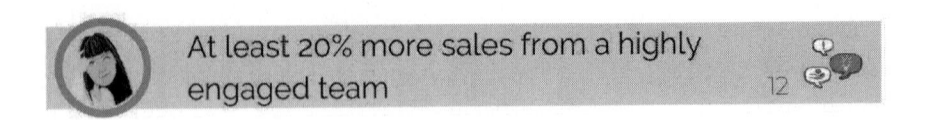

> At least 20% more sales from a highly engaged team 12

Emotioneering It

- ASK – Sit down with every person in your team and ask them what they are motivated by or what they are working towards.

- Remind – When communicating with your employees remind them of what they are working towards and why it makes a difference.

- Repeat – Understand that the motivational drivers will change over time and what someone wanted last year is not the same as it is now.

♥ ♥ ♥ ♥ ♥

Always Believe In Your Goal

♥

"Aim for the stars; hit the moon" is a phrase that I have lived my life by. Setting a big audacious goal or as Ziad Khoury, from Frontline Performance Group would say 'A big fat aspirational goal'. Elon Musk has proved sometimes it doesn't matter that you missed the goal what matters is how much you missed it by so you can go again. For example, promising a moon shot in 6 months and then it is delivered in 3 years. It still happened. Often when a goal is important enough people will do anything to make it happen even when the deadline may change.

I remember my optimism when I turned up at my mentoring call with Taran Hughes and announced that I was going to write this book in 2 weeks. He cheered me on, half knowing of course that this would be one hell of a BIG challenge and I might have bitten off more than I can chew by committing to two weeks. Needless to say, when I went back to our mentoring call a month later with my tail between my legs, we discussed the moon-shot approach and he reminded me that having 8,000 words down even if not the full 44,000 aim was more than most leaving only 36,000 to go. And here you are reading it... see, it did get done. Yey!

In the workplace, many targets are set based on the average or minimal performance that a company requires from their employees. The next time someone walks in and asks, "what's the top person achieving?" Let's not stifle their ambition with dismissive statements like "Don't try and run before you can walk". Tell them what the answer is and help them understand how to get there. Chances are they will get there and also exceed their monthly targets month on month because they are aiming for big fat hairy audacious goals.

Golf Blindfolded

The challenge is that without a goal being set you really are asking your team to play golf blindfolded and we all know how successful that would be (I bet the golf lovers are thinking of adding that as an activity for their next group trip). Coming back to the point here though is that if goals aren't set then the focus on performance will be low in comparison. In the workplace is that also goals could contradict the agenda for another department or business objective so it is key to ensure that they align.

Also, when it comes to budget goals the challenge can be that the team are set goals that just contribute to the overall number when there could be much more potential or even worse, new or underperforming team members are sometimes given lower targets than the average that is being achieved. Remember I mentioned earlier is essential to establish the potential and how much the seat/role is worth to the company and to the individual.

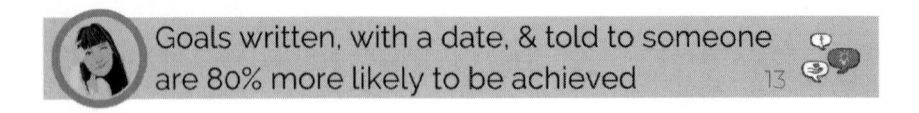

> Goals written, with a date, & told to someone are 80% more likely to be achieved   13

Emotioneering It

- Plan goal setting sessions every month in the diary with your people. As close to the start as possible.
- Schedule them in advance (some great leaders put them on the calendar at the start of the year)
- Do not change the date or time (unless it is an emergency)
- Remember it's about their potential more than it is about the company objectives.
- Ask illuminating questions
- Encourage them to set goals with deadlines/times. How many actions do you see without this?
- Ensure they are measurable and relevant
- Follow Up / Accountability. In the next month start with what was agreed in the previous month.

· ♥ · ♥ · ♥ · ♥ · ♥ ·

Rewards & Incentives

♥

Quite a few years back while working as a consultant a few of us were about to facilitate a customer service workshop for the day and take groups of 10 people each. So, we turned up super positive and ready to rock, only to be confronted with employees in tears, breaking their hearts. At first, we had no idea what had happened and we were very shocked.

We soon found out that the commission structure had changed suddenly which meant that some people lost all their commission and reward completely overnight. This industry was extremely lucrative and let's just say it wasn't a small amount. We received the backlash and pretty much had to throw the plan of the customer service workshop out the window and just listen and allow their emotions before passing feedback to the client.

My heart was breaking for them. Some couldn't pay rent; some had no way to make their bills that month, and for this change to happen so suddenly it really pulled on their emotions. They believed they had earned that money and deserved it so couldn't understand why this had happened. What had happened was that the company wanted to make a change to be more ethical, which they were well within their right to do and had been working on it for a while. The challenge was that they launched the change far too quickly to allow anyone to understand it, prepare for the change or get on the bus with it. It was like anarchy that day. Something I will never forget. Incentives and reward have been and will continue to be a large part of motivating people because it has the ability to change someone's life.

Opportunity Left On The Table

Is that the consistent level of salary can become part of expectation and is somewhat instant gratification. It is expected and delivered on a periodic basis. This can have a boost in productivity when someone is promoted or within the first 90 days of a new role. Another challenge can be that a commission structure could be capped which then means your best employees aren't motivated to keep going past a certain point.

Imagine that on some teams there are people stashing sales deals for the following week or next month because they know that there is no win for them as well as the company after a certain benchmark. Also, they could take their foot off the gas when they know that the goal is achieved halfway through the month when there is a world of opportunity out there being left on the table.

> 44% increase in sales when a strong incentive plan is in place 14

Emotioneering It

- It is one of the MOST motivating elements to an employee
- Make it uncapped
- Make sure there are levels or tiers to the plan. Like the steps on a ladder. This increases engagement further.
- For the managers bonused on whole team results add a caveat on one-to-one sessions being completed
- Think about the level of revenue you will keep and not what you are paying out

- Ensure that it has the ability to change their life or make a big difference.

♥ · ♥ · ♥ · ♥ · ♥

Gaining Buy-In

♥

In the UK there are many of us that enjoy watching a TV programme called Dragon's Den (the UK's version of Shark Tank). What is clear is that the way the person approaches their pitch really has a direct impact on whether they receive the right investment or gain anyone's buy-in to their idea. Shout out to Zineb Layachi and Taran Hughes co-founders of PitchSLAP, as they help entrepreneurs secure investment and I have attended their sessions a few times to hear their on-the-spot feedback to business owners. A lot of what is discussed in these sessions (they are incredible sessions by the way) is about the communication and the big purpose or why behind the business. "People don't' buy the what, they buy the why".

When I thought back to all those Dragon's Den episodes, I found this to be true. The ones with enthusiasm, communicated their offering clearly and articulated the 'why' seemed to get much better investment opportunities. The same can be said about decisions and ideas in the workplace. Are we articulating and educating them clearly and with why they should care about it. Think of team dislikes or negative comments as questions. They don't have the knowledge or understand why it benefits them. WIIFM – What's in it for me? Everyone's favourite radio station.

The next time you have to explain something reflect on whether you are explaining it from a what is it for the company perspective or are you taking the time to mention their motivational drivers and the impact that it will mean to them.

Getting People On The Bus

Imagine you have a great idea for the company, consult no one other than the senior leadership team. Then release the process change or kick off a new project by telling everyone what now needs to happen, only to find that there is a lack of engagement in the change followed by a lot of backlash from the team. The feedback you start to receive is that the change will not help or cause more problems. Hardly anyone likes to be told what to do and as a team, it is important that there is collaboration and involvement.

Even when receiving feedback and discussing potential options you do not have to guarantee that opinions or ideas will affect the decisions only that they will be considered when making changes. The challenge with anything new is that we can also consider the 'Law of diffusion of innovation', which means that there is only ever likely to be 13.5% of people that will be your champions and buy in to change straight away when the next 60% of people will need a little convincing. So ask yourself if you have explained to the team what is actually in it for them as well as the customer and business.

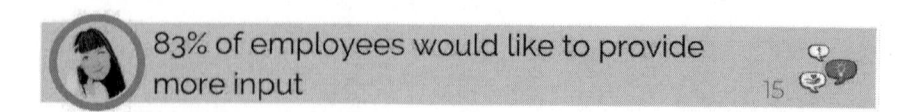

83% of employees would like to provide more input 15

Emotioneering It

- Involve the team in the decision-making process. You may have the final decision although the more involved they can be the better.
- Always communicate first about how it can benefit them (not you or the company)
- At the end of each week ask the team to complete a form with 3 elements, Highlights Challenges, Ideas / Suggestions.

Analytics Tools & Software

♥

It was 2015 remember being at a conference (yes, another one) as a performance consultant and seeing unveiled a new type of SAAS product that was going to truly be able to help frontline service companies, especially in hospitality and automotive. Padraig O'Connell was the CTO delivering the presentation and showing us the MVP (minimal viable product) of what is known as IN-Gauge today. There were about 150 consultants in the room at the time, I was sitting in the front and happened to glance around behind me. WOW! Everyone had started off sitting quite comfortably and laid back, now they were on the edge of their seats ALL leaning forward.

That's how engaged they were with the concept of IN-Gauge. Almost wanting to jump up and down with joy, ask a million questions or get up on the stage with Padraig. Ha! It was a sight to see and something that I wish I had been able to capture on video or image, of course, I was far too gripped just as everyone else was. The reason for this is that anyone that has worked in service, sales and performance management know how clunky excel sheets or software made in the 1980s /1990s that still controlled a lot of the data at many organisations was.

Many systems are archaic or even worse don't exist. Especially not in a way that engaged teams and made sense to them. IN-Gauge is the stuff dreams are made of. Even if it was an MVP, it was far better than any alternatives at that point. Today this superior software is revolutionising the workplace for many teams.

Knowing The Score

Imagine playing a game where you do not know the score or what it takes to win? How can you muster the belief and hope to keep going? Eventually, you would start to lose momentum, lose clarity, and start playing something else or give up altogether. This happens in the business world too.

Your team want to know where they are at, league tables, stats and other key performance metrics can help with this. It also helps with belief. If the team can see that one person can do it then it supports and fills up the belief that is possible for them too. From a learning perspective and with more and more remote workers making up teams, it is also crucial to be able to provide them with a way to learn where it does not have to be face to face in a classroom setting.

> Teams with moderate use of In-Gauge have an ave. increase of 323% in incremental revenue [6]

Emotioneering It

- Ensure you are tracking performance metrics and KPIs (Key Performance Indicators) especially for sales revenue. This can be tracked month on month, year on year as a total and broken down by employee. Check out IN-Gauge as mentioned earlier to see if there are benefits for your team. There is a world of CRM systems out there too, the challenge is finding one that provides a great user experience as well as keeping your team engaged.
- Visual Graphs are a great way to show the employee how well they are doing compared to target and the average

- Ensure you have a Learning Management System (LMS) - Check out Talent LMS – It's voted one of the best on the market and voted the easiest to use – go to https://www.talentlms.com/index/aff:mmg to sign up for free and get a free tutorial.
- Create a league table. For recognition driven employees this is motivational, and competitions can be coordinated based on this. As a side note, how you create the league table is extremely important as you want it to be as fair as possible. Choose metrics based on this.
- You could also have multiple league tables.
- Whilst 'people make numbers, numbers don't make people' the numbers don't often lie; these can be used to hold people accountable for their responsibilities.

Opportunities To Grow

I recently had the pleasure of reading the book The Pumpkin Plan by Mike Michalowicz. It's a great book and I highly recommend it. One of the key points that it talks about which turned on my human resources radar was the organisational chart. Mike talks about how we often do an organisational chart based on right now or the next 12 months rather than looking at the BEST possible option for you to achieve your overall company mission or goal.

For example, the Modern Mind Group's mission is 'Emotioneering to change the hearts and minds of at least one million people for the better', so if I take that One Million number and cast my visionary and strategic mind forward, what would the organisational chart look like at that point, then work backwards from that. It means that for every person you recruit you can plan their possible progression. This is succession planning and people strategy.

Employees want opportunities to grow. It is highly unlikely in the modern world that a person will get a job and stay in it for life and now many come to the interview asking about future opportunities. Are you planning for it?

Misconceptions of Learning

'If you keep doing what you've always done, you will only get what you have always got.' The landscape and dynamics of a market can change quite quickly and if the team aren't being developed, they won't be ready for it. This will lead you to wonder if they can deliver on what is required and potentially motivate you to start to look externally for someone when the right person could be right there in front of you. There can also be a perception that learning must be in the traditional methods which is only the tip of the iceberg and when we look more at the learning opportunities there can be so many more.

Remote working has certainly lifted the demand for eLearning solutions or virtual training which then presents itself again because the business may not have been ready for that change so quickly. Often a team are wanting to progress and grow for their life fulfilment but never have the opportunity. People overlooked for promotion or growth opportunities often immediately start looking elsewhere as it can really make them feel undervalued if they were not chosen.

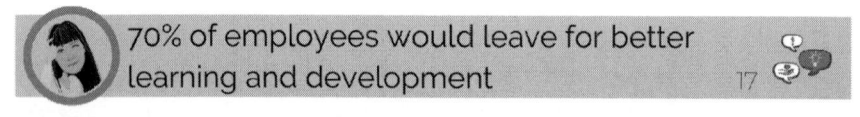

> 70% of employees would leave for better learning and development 17

Emotioneering It

- Inspire the 'Be Do Haves' over the 'Have Be Do's'. Don't wait until they are ready. Create a culture of fail fast, learn quickly.
- Look for those that are looking for more responsibility and empower them by delegating projects and activities.
- Promote more from within than externally
- When someone doesn't get a promotion that they are looking for clearly explain why and if it is based on experience then set out a plan of what they will require to do or demonstrate so that the next time the opportunity arises they are in a better position.

Surveys & Feedback

♥

"Oh no I don't want to send a survey out right now as we have some big business months ahead so I don't want to emotionally trigger the staff" – This is something that a client once said to me when I was suggesting that to plan for the next year, we really could do with having some anonymous feedback from the team. The thing is, they were already emotionally triggered. We always are. It's not about the timing of a survey, it's about the frequency and whether a company is asking for input and then acting upon that input. This company had never done a survey. They had asked for open feedback in discussions although the truth rarely comes out and then it isn't anonymous so it can't be taken as objectively.

I get that asking questions does lead to more work, of course, it does, because now you have some challenges to fix, things to change although it's better than using pie in the sky thinking and not asking anyone for their input before planning the next steps. Gallup reports that world-class engagement starts at about 36%, when I read this my jaw nearly hit the floor. The teams that I have worked with, and we are talking about the best of the best, have had at least 80% engagement. There really is a world of potential out there when you know how to achieve it.

Assumptions Make...

Often many people in life will assume or guess what other people think and how they feel. These assumptions can be determined by our life experiences our interpretations and our beliefs. This happens a lot in business too, even when trying to understand what the customers want. We could just speak to the current customers and learn from them.

When it comes to employees they want to be heard and based on the 4 big human needs listening to them will increase their sense of value and that they belong. That is unless you do nothing with the information you receive. This can also be a secondary challenge. When you take the time to send a survey let's ensure there is action on the back of it. Another challenge can be that you might ask the questions without anonymity which can affect the answers that are received. Allowing anonymity allows the business leader to stay rational and focus on what is there in black and white.

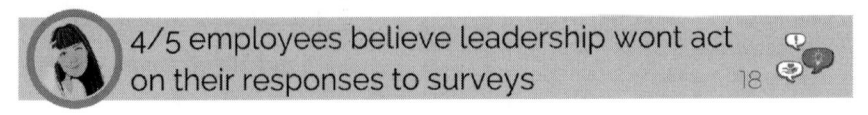

> 4/5 employees believe leadership wont act on their responses to surveys 18

Emotioneering It

- At least twice a year for an employee engagement survey
- Facilitated by a third party if possible or a separate department
- Make it anonymous to encourage more honesty and it will help you stay focused on being objective and rational.
- Ensure feedback is shared with managers and employees
- Use the feedback as an opportunity to respond back and be transparent about the future of the company.

Products & Prices

♥

When was the last time you walked into a car dealership and demanded to see the full spec sheet for the car that you were buying? Oh, that's right, 98% of you probably said 'never'. That's because it's not the customer's job to be overwhelmed by this information it is the sales and service team's job to know them and the difference so that they can make presentations about the elements that really matter to that person. Features tell benefits sell (I'm sure you've heard this one before somewhere). The expectation for a service and salesperson to have extremely strong knowledge should be high. It builds their belief in the products and builds their credibility to be able to know the answers when a customer asks the questions. They can easily paint an experience for the customer to visualise or synthetically feel. Do your team really know your products?

From a pricing perspective You can walk into a car dealership, and they will have the new fan dangled, high spec, kitted out car right in front of you – this is the showroom, the best they can offer you will be right in front of you, on top of everything else, although not everyone goes for this one. That's retail for you.

Take your local supermarket store and you are looking for cookies. Luxury cookies are often on the top shelf, at eye level and the premium cookies at your waist, then the economy or budget cookies at the bottom, which you have to bend for. Which do you think they sell more of? Have you got a tiered structure for your pricing and do you take a top-down approach?

Get Them Familiar

The challenge can be that when the team aren't encouraged to know more about the products and therefore perform badly when it comes to sales because they will end up only promoting what they know, which will lose credibility or trust from the customer when they do not know the answers to their questions or appear nervous with their offer. You may have great products and services although the customers will never understand them if the team aren't able to educate them. This leaves customers unable to make an informed buying decision. The revenue and your product conversion can be directly impacted by the way your team and customers feel about them.

When working in travel I would be involved in what they called FAM trips. FAM stood for familiarisation trips, these were for employees to test out the facilities, experience what the customers would feel, give quality feedback to the partners and clients as well as be able to be confident about that place and the specific facilities to customers. I had the opportunity to go on many of these and they were incredible, did I make more sales as a result? Absolutely! Plus, the venues had a new brand ambassador and to this day friends and family still call to ask me about hotels and locations they are considering.

In automotive it would be test drives, car shows and hospitality it would be room tours. Any way that the employees could connect to the products and services much better.

Employees performed 87% higher than those who had not had product training 19

Emotioneering It

- Customers and clients are looking for New Mechanisms – Basically, products or processes bundled up into something presentable to market.

- Give your employees opportunities to package different products together with some price flexibility to use at their discretion.

- Don't underestimate the power of belief. Often when a product doesn't generate a large amount of revenue compared to others then it could be that the sales team don't believe in it or aren't offering your other products to best serve your customers and clients.

- Have a tiered approach to your products with a retail mindset, Luxury, Premium, Low Cost. It gives an opportunity to follow a top-down presentation approach.

- Give the team time and experiences that allow for familiarisation of the products and services. This will increase their confidence therefore making the employees advocates of those products and services. They could also give you valuable feedback to improve what you offer.

What's On Your Mind?

♥

✶ Ring ring, ring ring* I glance at the phone feeling apathetic and slightly down, I think to myself 'what do they want now? They only call me when they want something'. I pick up the phone only to receive the chit chat from my boss before they quickly move on to what they really called about and what they need. I sigh when I put down the phone and think 'why does everything feel so objective?'

You might have this happen a lot to you in the workplace or with family and friends. It's often when our emotional or 'big human needs' are not being met. When we don't get the opportunity to express ourselves, our true emotions or say exactly what's on our minds. A lot of work communication is done very transactionally leaving very little room to grow the relationship or provide space for truthful conversations. This happened many times for me in a few companies and I was also one of those leaders at first, less empathy more 'get the job done' which did nothing for my reputation I can tell you that much.

I suppose once you've learned the lesson to allow for non-work-related conversations to take place, to make an effort to build relationships as well as deliver outcomes then you see the magic that it truly can bring to a team and the impact on the person.

Affection Vs Objection

In a business that has a high focus on performance and less on relationships, leaders and workers can often feel guilty about having conversations that are not 'productive' or business-related. A conversation just about someone's life or their feelings can be seen as not necessary. This can cause teams to have a barrier to building great relationships and in a remote world, it is less likely that these types of non-objective interactions take place. This means it is also less likely for employees to have a best friend at work which Gallup found was a contributing factor to remaining in a company. Employees can end up feeling like a number and isolated. This will affect productivity, engagement and is very likely to contribute to a high turnover of staff.

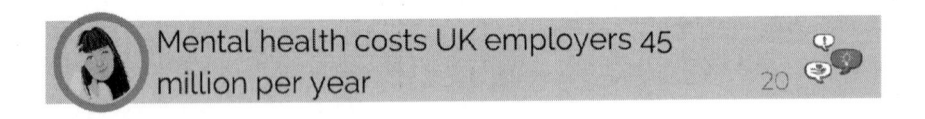

> Mental health costs UK employers 45 million per year
> 20

Emotioneering It

- Have a non-objective one2one with your employees at least once per month.
- Ask them "what's on your mind?" and wait for their response.
- Remember emotions and thoughts do not come out in order. It is not a business agenda where we take minutes. Once they are expressed then the order can be found.
- Stay positive and aim not to ask "why?" often people don't know why they feel a certain way so it can cause them to feel stupid and close up. Stick to 'what and how' questions.
- Use supportive and reassuring statements vs. dismissive statements. For example, "I know you can get through this" vs "don't be silly". Whatever they are expressing is a big deal to them. Aim to empathise.

- Check out the theory on Transactional Analysis by Eric Berne in the 1950s it will help to understand how to respond and how conflict can occur. Many people only learn one way of communicating so when something happens to a person, they aren't prepared on how to adapt their approach. I use this theory in practice often.

•♥•♥•♥•♥•♥•

Accountability

♥

"I would love for you to understand how this happened so please listen to the call recording and then once both of us have listened to it we can discuss it" I said to a girl on my team. On hearing me say this Naomi let out a cry, threw herself on the floor and sobbed. A response that I was not expecting and behaviour I hadn't seen before. Naomi had been generating complaints from customers due to their non-empathetic approach as well as lacking emotional intelligence. I had resolved every single one until this point, I had decided that it was time for a new approach to help Naomi see what was happening and learn from it. The reaction I had not accounted for.

The easy thing would have been to say ok and leave it go although it wasn't fair on the customers, the team, my time, or the company reputation. Most of all it wasn't fair on Naomi to help her grow and evolve in her career. I gave her two options, go take a break and when ready come back and listen to the call or go home for the rest of the day and listen to the call tomorrow. I explained why this was important and eventually Naomi plucked up the courage to face the situation and listen to the call. After which we were able to discuss the feedback, reduce the perception gaps and ensure a plan of action that meant there were fewer complaints of this nature in the future. Great, you might think, job done! Wait for it.

6 months later I was no longer working with her, when I ended up going for social drinks to catch up, she said to me " It's just not the same without you around anymore, today I had to take a complaint from a customer about another member of the team then go investigate, listen to the call and then give them and their manager the feedback" My jaw dropped and then I started to smile and replied " Looks like you don't need me around, after all, you haven't only reduced your own complaints you're now helping resolve other peoples, I'm so happy for your progress Naomi, well done!" she responded "Oh yeah! I hadn't even thought about that". She went on to land a great job for a large organisation and had her own team to lead too. The point I am making here is that accountability is not convenient or a fun part of being a leader although it is necessary for the growth of individuals and the business. What you allow will continue.

Accountability is Engaging

We are all motivated by accountability. It can help keep us engaged. It's the reason I have consultants and coaches that support what I do too. There are a few sides to accountability. From the employee side when there is little or no accountability it can lead to people not taking processes procedures or rules seriously. The best performers will become unmotivated when they know that they are doing their job and doing it well when there are others that are on the team that are not supporting the overall success of the team or organisation. The challenge from a leader's perspective is knowing what to say and when to draw the line. It's good to understand though that accountability has a scale from informal to formal or disciplinary action. Many people only think of as a formal process.

When accountability is only used in a formal way and as the only way to move the needle then it can increase the pressure and contribute to a toxic fearful environment. It is about finding the balance. The full emotioneering business blueprint provides this balance because it looks at the other engagement and cultural aspects alongside the accountability. Then a challenge can be, from a remote perspective, that because a leader is not with the person to assess competence, how can they then hold someone accountable for something that they cannot always see happening?. Of course, give trust although let's be honest, that trust can be broken at times.

> 47% of workers received feedback 'a few times or less a year' from their managers 21

Emotioneering It

- Inspect what you expect. Having regular check ins or site visits can help you to understand what is happening.
- Audit the process from a quality perspective
- Get a second opinion
- What you allow will continue. Be responsive and not reactive by planning how to approach the situation then following through on it.
- Are you/they part of the problem or are they part of the solution?
- Know the intention of accountability is not to judge a person it is to move them forward in their potential and their life. They are being held accountable for the behaviours and responsibilities that they agreed and committed to.
- Give opportunity for improvement
- Provide support if it is necessary. A lack of support will not help them to get to their potential.
- There must be accountability for poor performance and behaviour because the rest of the team deserve that. Not holding someone accountable is going to affect the whole culture of your team.
- Document your process

· ♥ · ♥ · ♥ · ♥ · ♥ ·

Four

Activities

♥

The Winning Combination

As part of people operations, there are a lot of activities that can take place on a periodic basis. All these touchpoints, for example, time spent with your team, the delivery and consistency of them provide the winning combination. Being a leader of people is a visual job. Too many times a leader can be found in a back office or taking a convenient option for them like sending an email regarding feedback versus having one to one time with them.

The performance magic will really start to happen when a leader spends time with their team. It's just not good enough for your team to think 'oh my managers really busy' or 'they have more important things to do'. When you sign up to be a leader of people then there is going to be a lot of work and effort that goes into that. Not just once at the start. It is a revolving process of activities that help drive the performance.

You might be reading this, rolling your eyes and thinking, 'Yeah right! There aren't enough hours in a day Melissa!'. What I would say to that is 1) It's about prioritisation, not how busy you are 2) setting boundaries and saying no to the things that are not going to have the biggest impact 3) Do you even know exactly where you spend your time?

I recently met a wonderful businesswoman and someone I am proud to call a friend. That lady is Abigail Barnes.

Abigail is the creator of the 888 Formula and the author of Time Management for Entrepreneurs & Professionals. I highly suggest you check it out. On-Page 16 Abigail unveils her 5 Step Process for Turning Your Time into Productivity.

The first thing to do is a Time Audit for 7 Days. Write down everything that you do and how long it takes for a week and then review it. It's easy for me to say 50 -70% of your working time I recommend to spend with your team (if you have a large team otherwise this might be overkill with 2-3 employees) although until you see where you are currently spending your time it will be difficult to see how or admit that you are not with them enough.

Many leaders want to know, how often to spend time with their team, what and how to do certain activities. In this chapter, I will share it all.

The smart activities that I share with you in this chapter are absolutely the ones that will move the needle as well as goal-setting sessions which I talked about in the last chapter when helping people to be more engaged. Get your time audit done then plan these into your calendar as non-negotiable.

Where there is a will, there is a way!

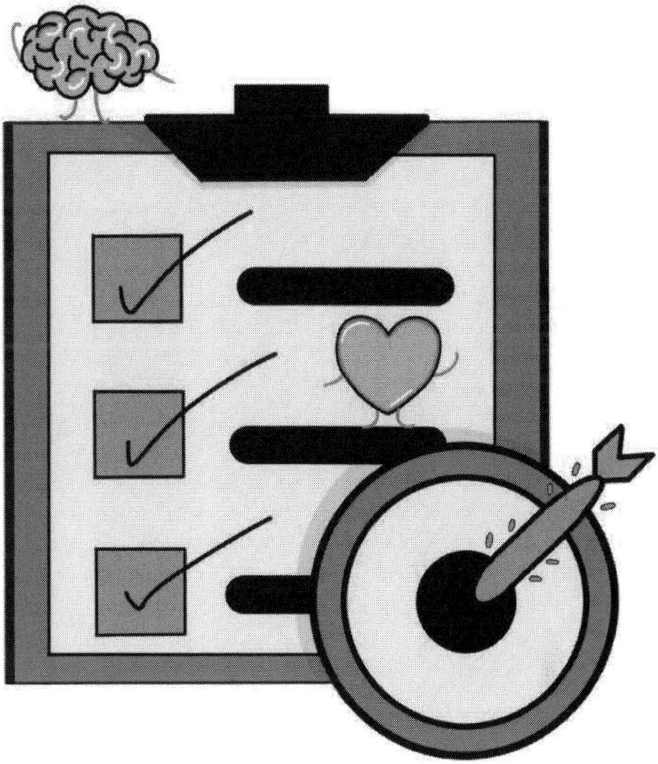

Analysis & Data

Over the years as a people operations and performance consultant, there were many times when I would ask questions such as "What was the highest revenue per month?" or "What's your conversion percentage on that product?" as well as "What's the best month you have ever had?" often to be met by blank faces quickly followed by the sentence "Well I think it was XYZ, I'll just call (insert person's name) to get them to figure it out for us".

These situations have been across communication with executive leaders, middle managers, or even frontline employees on their own performance. This could be because they aren't being given the data or they aren't having the data explained to them in a way that makes it memorable and it's quite possible they don't know why it makes a difference. The difference is knowing this can provide people with social proof.

There really are only two ways to increase belief, first is with stories, people will say "wow great story, but is it really true?" that's where the social proof comes in and secondly 'showing' what is possible. This could be done with data, statistics, live demonstrations, videos or recordings. When you provide people with social proof their belief goes up and they will have an "ah-ha" moment. Just remember "people make numbers, numbers don't make people"

The Data of The Beast

As a business grows so does the data. Many start, with a whiteboard, a website, an excel sheet and a bank account. Then every person that is added to the team, every new customer, every new product, every new service, and the repeat business all adds to the data and metrics that make up the performance of a company.

Potential isn't just about things feeling like they are going ok, it's about knowing exactly what the performance is now so you can plan a strategy back from where you want to be. Not knowing where you are at also won't help you to appreciate the journey of how far you have come, which will mean you have a negative bias in planning forward. To help others believe, you have to believe too and that comes with having full clarity on your analysis. There is also a challenge in who will be responsible for keeping track of the data and reporting on it as well as knowing what software and systems to use.

> Poor data can cost businesses 20%–35% of their operating revenue 22

Emotioneering It

- Start tracking the numbers today and appoint at least one person to champion the collection of the data, If you haven't already.

- When I say numbers, these are your key metrics and they could be leads, conversions, revenue, NPS (net promoter score), retention rates, visitors, follow-ups or calls.

- Look over the last 12 months to know what the performance was for each month. If you have 24 months of data, then that's even better. This will show you some of the trends and seasonality of the business.

If you haven't already done this then do it for sales. An accounts balance is not enough.

- Next split the revenue into different products/revenue streams to know where it is coming from

- Take this down to employee level for each member of the team and month. If they have been given a target then mark if it was over or under it. This will give you a snapshot of the most consistent team members vs the not so consistent. (if they have not been given a target start developing a plan to introduce them)

- Create a league table of employees as well as locations if you have more than one and different areas you cover. This will increase competition and create more engagement.

- If all this sounds long and overwhelming, then a performance consultant or data analyst can help you. Think of skilled people in googlesheets, excel, tableau, numbers, and systems. The more visual you can make it for people the better. KPI dashboards and CRM systems will help to support this.

- Ensure that the data is updated daily, weekly and monthly

The Biggest Impact

♥

I remember a time when I was supporting a client manager to implement one to ones with their team. I'd been waiting for around two weeks to receive the calendar invites, to observe them and provide feedback on some of the first ones with the team. After a call with the business owner and a gentle nudge from the internal champion we finally got them booked in and scheduled. Mark had always spent the day in, day out with his team so couldn't really understand why it made a difference to schedule a one to one with them and support with feedback.

Once Mark initiated the one to ones he instantly saw the difference and thanked me for supporting him to complete them. He had been worried about their reaction or what would come up on the sessions. What he realised was that this was a valuable time to be able to discuss openly the successes and challenges of individual performance as well as allow them to express themselves. In a group discussion, there is less openness and less impact because it isn't dedicated one to one time based on that individual person. This is where the biggest impact and changes are always seen. Fast forward Mark has been promoted himself, some of his teams have also been promoted into leadership roles and he now is an advocate of one to ones with employees.

One Bird One Stone

We often don't know or realise the impact of the one to one time with people. It can be overlooked and for convenience, leaders can choose group sessions or team discussions using the 'two birds one stone' approach. This is where trust and openness are not going to be fostered because people often fear standing out from the crowd or truly expressing their vulnerability. Sure, there will be some people that will express themselves regardless of a group setting or not. This personality type makes up only 5-10% of most teams. It can be higher if the team have worked together for a long time although they will still want your attention. When leaders realise the power of spending one to one time with their teams the magic really starts to happen, and it is where the biggest behaviour changes are seen.

#1 Sign of a good 1-2-1 is safe, open & honest communication (employees surveyed) 23

Emotioneering It

- Ensure that you or your line managers are spending time with each team member on a one-to-one basis at least once per week.

- Use open questions to see where they are at. What their thoughts are and what support they need.

- Relationships come first so make sure you have a strong relationship before giving any constructive feedback.

- Remind them of their goals and encourage each employee to take action

The Morning Rally

Have you ever been into your favourite retail store early in the morning to see them huddled together in the corner of the store and wondered what they were doing? This is what I call in the service-based industry the Morning Rally. Have you ever heard of the phrase "Burn the boats"? I was introduced to this phrase by Drake Beil who quoted it as he was delivering a keynote speech at a conference.

It originally comes from 1519 when a Spanish expedition led by Hernan Cortes landed in Mexico. Knowing his team were already exhausted from the journey he ordered the boats be burned at the shore so that they knew there was no chance to return, so would focus on accomplishing the mission and go forward.

This is one of the ideas of the Morning Rally, although a little bit less severe, the employees can still get in their cars to go home, I am not suggesting burning them. Ha! It's more about helping them put yesterday out of focus, to leave what's been and gone, learn from it and focus on the day ahead (Although I'm sure many of the frontline employees in service-based industries would say it is a real battle at times).

Don't Miss An Opportunity To Reset

The team have started their day and are already having reservations about how successful it will be or they haven't yet got over what happened the day before. Feeling a little lost and not yet ready they are about to face your customers. This is a missed opportunity to hit the reset or wave the metaphorical chequered flag to emotioneer team focus.

From a leader's perspective, they might be thinking a few things. Firstly, they could be nervous or feel like imposters to deliver a talk to the team. Jennifer Louise CEO of the Successful Salon Club mentions on the Emotioneering podcast episode about how she used to talk to herself in the mirror before approaching the team in the morning to boost her self esteem and shake off the imposter syndrome. This was early on in her career now Jennifer Louise is an international speaker.

Secondly, It could be that you or your leaders don't see the value in team talks and think they are repeating themselves. From a third perspective, they could think they are too busy or feel undervalued themselves to want to prioritise the team talks. The 'I'll do it later' thought often becomes never. Lastly, the remote, hybrid workplace or shift patterns could make it more challenging although this is a barrier so where there is a will, there is a way.

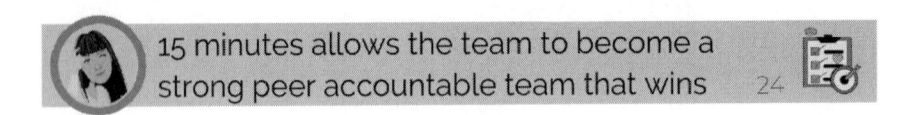

> 15 minutes allows the team to become a strong peer accountable team that wins 24

Emotioneering It

- Make it a daily morning rally. If it is a 7-days per week business and leaders have a few days off, then encourage them to start it on the days they are in work then once into a rhythm encourage another supervisor to deliver the morning rally on the days that they are not in.

- Look at the performance from the previous day and firstly find the positives. Even if it was a difficult day there will be some. Use it as a chance to give recognition to employees for a job well done based on results, behaviours, or attitude.

- Explain the game plan for the day, what is coming ahead and remind them of the team goal as well as how far ahead or behind they are. This is also an ideal time to talk about any competitions or incentives that are in play.

- Use it as a learning opportunity with a motivational statement, story, or statistic.

- Record by video or audio and write up the notes then distribute them to anyone that missed it or as a reminder. Even better you could share the video or the soundtrack.

The Power of The Town Hall

♥

In 1921 in New York the Town Hall was opened. It was started by a group of suffragists wanting to have a meeting place to educate the people and have open discussions on topics of the day. It was after the 19th Amendment was passed which allowed women the right to vote. It did not matter about your public status as it was built in a way that there was "not a bad seat in the house" everyone had a clear view and could participate.

The UK also followed suit in the 19th century and either a Town Hall or Municipal Building were available for promoting and enhancing the quality of life for the community. Let's call it, regardless of what side of the pond you are on, a building to discuss and support the people. Many executive leaders now adopt this approach or concept as part of their business operations to hold discussions on a periodic basis to help educate their people on the company strategy and performance as well as hold an open forum to open for questions and discussions.

This allows them to stay close to the pulse of the team and know what is really happening on the frontline. In my time as a learning and performance consultant, I have been invited to many client town hall sessions or asked by them to help set up Town Hall sessions by sharing the best-in-class example of how a Town Hall can be run for the greatest impact.

Missing The Message

Senior managers or the executive team may not know if the strategy and objectives are clearly being communicated with the frontline employees and the frontline employees do not fully know that their concerns, ideas, and suggestions are being passed on from their line manager, especially if changes are not seen straight away.

Employees could also feel very disconnected from the overall company view if it is a very large organisation. Some of the most inspirational people in the organisation are also at the executive level where the employees don't get the interaction on a day-to-day basis, especially if the senior leader has worked there for many years and are part of how the company has grown. When there is not an opportunity to hear strategy and to know the senior leaders care about hearing from their team it can lead to people working in silos or being disengaged with their work. Leaders may not feel they are backed up by senior leadership because they are always the ones fighting the good fight and being a sounding board for the team.

> 74% prefer a collaborative culture instead of the manager making all the decisions 25

Emotioneering It

- Aim to run a town hall session at least every 6 months
- Plan a presentation with the support of the line managers including objectives and results.
- Ask the employee for some questions in advance to share as part of a presentation, this will then also encourage others to speak up on the day.
- Aim not to fear the uncomfortable questions. If you as a leader do not know the answer that is ok and say so. Your team don't expect

you to have all the answers they do expect to be heard, to be taken seriously and to be told the truth.

- Get as many of the team at the session as possible.
- If it can't be done in person then a virtual option is better than not at all.

Training Your People

♥

The only way a person is going to develop and improve is if they learn new skills or are trained in a new area of expertise. Fostering a culture of curiosity and growth is key to growing your organisation, having a highly engaged team and world-class results. There is that old quote you may have heard of "What if we train them well and they leave? What if we don't and they stay?" The corporate dilemma. Richard Branson is also quoted as saying, "Train people well enough so they can leave, treat them well enough so they don't want to". I love both.

When I run my workshop a few times a year, L&P for SME (Learning & Performance for Small to Medium Enterprises) what I ensure to go through is the preconceptions of learning, what we often think of is classroom training, formal qualifications, courses (tip of the iceberg) when in fact there is a much wider scope including podcasts, events, seminars, reading books, shadowing others in another department.

Creating A Learning Culture

Only 25% of what we hear is retained from courses or classroom training. This is why repetition and further learning followed by practical application is essential. 'Training is done by the training department' is something you will often hear in the business world when that is not the full picture of what brings about long-lasting changes.

In smaller companies, the challenge can be that they do not have a HR manager or training manager to delegate this to so they must become the responsibility of the owner or line manager. If the leader is not a continuous learner with a growth mindset this can immediately be a barrier as they won't often encourage others to adopt a flexible and curious approach to learning. Also, just because they know how to do something a leader may not have stepped back enough to look at 'the how' ie. the process of what they do and why they do it, to pass on that skill.

Then making sure there is time for learning is a big challenge because the service industry can be demanding. There also comes a point when there is also an expectation that a candidate takes responsibility for their learning, for example about products, sales scripts, processes it is in their interest to learn and practice which does require some discretionary effort when they join.

> Learners retain 10% they read, 25% of what they hear and 90% they teach back 26

Emotioneering It

- Identify from the metrics and the conversations about behaviour which are the immediate area of opportunity from this analysis.
- Assess the K.A.S.H. for each employee. Knowledge, Attitude, Skills and Habits.
- Encourage deliberate practice for any skills that are to be mastered.
- Curation Vs Creation. With a low budget and lack of resources, there are options to curate learning content rather than creating from scratch. This isn't saying that bespoke learning content that is evergreen isn't worth investing in, it's just that it's going to take time and your people need support on this today. So whether it is directing

them to podcasts, articles, YouTube videos. Whether you run a short workshop on why and how you do something as long as it is helping them move the needle on their performance and learning, that is what matters.

Observations

♥

Many years ago, I was observing Justine who was on my team, she had the longest average calls times with customers, had brilliant feedback scores and was one of the best teammates anyone could wish for. High metrics in every area apart from her conversion rate and revenue figures. As a sales consultant in the travel industry, there were high expectations of Justine to deliver on targets. I had chosen to spend some time with her side by side and listen to some calls being made.

What I found out from that was that Justine had incredible product knowledge on almost every service we could offer. The challenge was in closing the sale and encouraging the customer to make the booking. After a few tweaks and some roleplay later, Justine was performing much better. So much so that she ended up finishing in the top 10 of employees for that year in the company. I was delighted and there was never a more deserving person.

We observe people all the time. When we are at a restaurant and the server interacts with us, the person at the check-in desk at the hotel, or the flight attendant on the plane. How much attention do you pay to the way they serve you? Do they wow you? When was the last time someone left a lasting impression on you for incredible service? I bet you could tell me all the times you had bad service, extremely vividly. You might be the type of person that does this a lot although are you doing it with your own team? When did you last spend time just watching and listening to them?

Catch Them Doing Something Right

Mystery shoppers, executive visits, audits or big complaints happen all the time. Leaders can feel the big gulp due to the nerves kicking in when these happen, or the frustration sets in. The challenge can be that leaders don't realise that by changing habits to ensure they observe their team more that they won't have to worry about any of those things.

Are you a back-office manager? Do you send emails and pass on many messages when you could be out spending time observing your team, interacting with customers, and knowing what is happening first-hand?

When a manager spends more time in the back office and less time with their team there is a big challenge. A people leader is recommended to spend 50 - 70% of their time front of house with the people and knowing what is going on versus 30%- 50% back of house. You can't know the areas to improve without being there to observe different situations.

> 89% of customers who switch do so because of poor service and quality 27

Emotioneering It

- Firstly, communicate with your team that you care enough to know what they do and how they do things. You want to catch them doing something great so that you can share best practices with the team or wider company.

- Start with the team members who respond well to this information. When they have a positive experience, they will tell others.

- Block out some time to spend with each team member. To observe them in action. If you have a remote team, ask them to invite you to their next client meeting, or to have you on zoom whilst they make sales calls. Of course, they may be more nervous than usual, so reassure them about why you are doing this, for them, for the customer and for the company.

- Write notes on what you observe so that you have them recorded. Even if your mind points out the opportunities to improve first, through our negative bias, then also ensure that you list all the positives. They are there. They may seem obvious, but they are extremely important.

·♥·♥·♥·♥·♥·

Coaching Your Team

♥

A few months before starting to write this book Lucy Philip CEO of Purposefully Blended and I decided to create a workshop on Coaching with Olympic Energy. Inspired by the Tokyo Olympics. When researching, one of the key sports coaches I came across was Dean Boxall the Australian Swim Coach, also known as the coach that went viral for his Rock Star celebration when Ariana Titmus won gold. The thing is there are many layers to Dean Boxall. I started watching his coaching videos on YouTube and thought "WOW!". When you start to look at the way he coaches the team it really is a balance between a coaching style, directive leadership, enthusiasm, relatability, compassion, and inspiration. His analogies from batman sitting in a coffee shop to many more are memorable and allow his team to really connect. When breaking down his communication style it is very much about reminding the team of their motivational drivers and that isn't ever far from his language. In the world, there is this misunderstanding of what a coach is and what a coaching style is.

Often people separate sports coaching, workplace coaching, lifestyle coaching and training. When in reality it is about finding that combination in the middle. I ran a personal training and sports massage business for years and whilst we learn the technicalities and the theory, no one really teaches you how to communicate with your clients to bring the best out of them. That's what makes the difference between a great coach and a not-so-great coach.

Coaching is about helping someone grow and learn without teaching them or directing them to do something. It's about asking the right questions to draw out of people the action that they want to take. It's also about giving feedback in a way that is received as empowering and not painful. You can poke someone in the eye, or you can go slowly and touch the whole eyeball without any pain.

Are you Really Coaching?

Many leaders believe that they are coaching their teams when in reality this is not the case. This is because they often don't know the difference between coaching, directing, mentoring, and teaching. This can mean leaders end up just saying what to improve on and not highlighting the positives. When providing feedback on opportunities to improve the message can make a person feel reprimanded rather than taking it as constructive. Another barrier that can arise when a leader does attempt to coach is that there can be a lack of trust due to the manager not being congruent or not competent themselves.

A leader sometimes can get into a cycle of only coaching those that are underperforming or overperforming rather than equal time across the team. They can feel that over performers don't need their help, or they could feel nervous about coaching people with more challenging personalities. Getting the approach and balance right can see incredible results or changes from a team.

> Employees are 40% more engaged and give 38% more effort with effective coaching   28

Emotioneering It

Coaching is about helping someone unlock their potential from within.

- Build a relationship first – 'People do not care how much you know until they know how much you care!' John C Maxwell.
- Know what motivates them by asking the employees on your team. Everyone will be different, and they will change over time so keep checking.
- Ask them what they want to achieve or support them through illuminating questions to find their goal.
- Actively listen and check back your understanding
- Use encouraging statements and focus on the positives more than the opportunities.
- If someone cries, then pause, give them time, however long is required, then wait for them to speak again.
- Aim to close perceptions gaps and know that some people behave in a way that makes it difficult to coach. Remain patient and give them time. Not everyone will evolve at the same speed.
- Record a session to listen back to your language and questioning skills. Also, use a timer to assess how long you are speaking for in the session as you would want to majority to be coming from them.

Strategy Meetings

♥

Once upon a time in the business world, there was a CEO that was unhappy about the way the management were misaligned and didn't often collaborate. They decided to get everybody together for an activity. Every person was handed a marker pen and the same-coloured ball. They were asked to write their name on it and then throw it into the ball pit. Once that was complete there was now 60 of them and the team were asked to find the ball again with their name on it. So off they went, with a lot of noises of frustration, a few nudges and disgruntled managers that couldn't get near enough at first, 20 minutes later they all had the ball with their name on.

The CEO asked them to throw the balls back in the pit and said to them to lift the first ball they found and take it to that person. So off they went again and this time it only took 5 minutes for all 60 managers to receive the ball with their name on it. He then said "Now do you see the power of working together and collaboration? Many of you were grateful for the other person handing you the one with your name on as well as being happy that you finished in a much better time". The moral of the story is when we are all out in the field with our own agenda, working in silos can really affect the overall business output.

Don't Go Off Course

When there is no strategy meeting in place for the senior team there are a few risks to the business. Misalignment and a lack of teamwork due to silos mean that the customers and employees get treated differently which will be seen from the fluctuation of results. There will be a lack of understanding on multiple levels, less belief that the objectives are possible, lack of urgency towards company goals, lack of importance and a lack of strong results. Giving structure to a strategy meeting, making it periodic and providing statistics as well as sharing best practices will help to keep the mission on track. For the delivery of the meeting from the leader there are some pitfalls for example being too generic about the performance and not being able to articulate trends, explain the narrative behind the numbers or inspire their senior team can leave them feeling flat and disengaged. Remember to explain what, why and the how.

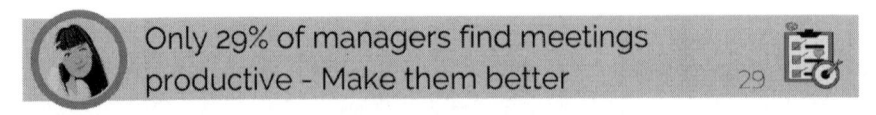

> Only 29% of managers find meetings productive - Make them better

Emotioneering It

- Plan them for the same time in the diary each month and aim not to move them.

- Ensure that the data and the blueprint or roadmap for the business strategy are set as a presentation template to walk through each time.

- Use graphs and visuals to identify the trends, making it clear when you talk about the narrative.

- Ensure that the actions and follow up comes first in the presentation from the last meeting

- Appoint someone to take minutes and share within 24 hours

♥ • ♥ • ♥ • ♥ • ♥

Team Meetings

♥

Much like the story I just shared here about the strategy meeting on a senior leadership level, the individual teams, and local communities within the organisation matter just as much. I remember being sent to Ireland for observation and assessment of a service and sales team. I made sure to speak to every team member that worked there on the day of my visit. That was front of house staff and back office.

When I asked them what their individual target was 95% could tell me exactly without hesitation. When I asked them what the team goal was 100% of them responded with a blank stare followed by a few saying, "do we have one?" or "I don't think that matters really". You see this was the culture that had been set up. Almost every member of the team was approaching their work as if they were flying solo.

Are They Flying Solo

This is a Top-down effect. If there is no strategy meeting at a senior level, the enthusiasm to hold one with the team won't be passed down to the local level. If you want teamwork, then a monthly team meeting can support the collaboration and help the team to understand how important they are to the whole process. The challenge can be to ensure these are planned and structured.

Leaders can often lose out waiting for the perfect time or for 100% of the team to be there when this will really stall progress. If 90% of the team can be there, then go ahead. Not having the right data or not being aware of individual performance can lead a team meeting to be very generic and not give the impact that is desired. The mood and behaviour of the leader matter. If the leader is pessimistic and doesn't transfer hope, trust and confidence then the team could end up feeling less confident than they came to the meeting with. It's worth looking at the language and tone of the meeting as well as the content.

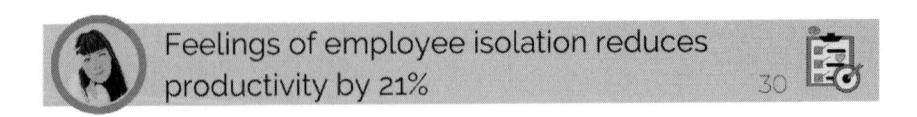

> Feelings of employee isolation reduces productivity by 21%   30

Emotioneering It

- Schedule team meetings at least once per month for up to 60 mins.
- Set a framework or agenda for the meeting. The info will be very similar to the morning rally only on a larger scale.
- Ask for input in advance from the team and encourage them to share at the meeting.
- Update them with as much transparency as you possibly can. Address their concerns.
- Share performance history and current performance with them. If you can show them where the team ranks on a local league table.
- Record and save 'best in class performance' for example the highest ever sale and by who.
- Brush up on your presenting skills and ask for feedback from peers or your own leader to give you opportunities for improvement.
- Use it as an opportunity to check the employees understanding of policies, procedures, or techniques.
- Set up an employee of the month award and ask each team member to vote for one of their colleagues and to explain why. The leadership team also have a vote each. The person who receives the most votes gets

a certificate and public recognition. I often get asked what if they win for a few months running, then that is fine. It will encourage others to step up and appreciate what it takes to be at the top.

Halfway Catchups

♥

There is a great book called 'When' By Daniel Pink and it really helped change my perspective on *When* we get things done as well as the magic at the *mid-point*. I highly suggest you read it. It puts procrastination in a whole new light. In the book, Daniel Pink mentions a researcher called Carrie Gersick who studied human beings in the corporate world although in different industries.

The groups were across, health care, banking, computer science and they were given 34 days to a deadline for a project. Management teams were stating that there were 4 stages that groups worked on projects and that they moved through them in this way, so Carrie Gersick decided to video them to see on a granular level what the stages were like. What was discovered was this was not the case of course there were inconsistencies and differences between the group although more astonishingly regardless of the group of people they didn't seem to get much done at all in the first half of the project, then come day 17 the groups went at record speed towards delivering the work to the deadline for day 34.

Carrie Gersick called this is "Uh Oh Effect". Fascinating! So think about your team and the halfway point in the month. I'm sure that they have done some of the work although do they accelerate towards the end of the month and turn up the gears? I'm sure with your help they certainly all can.

Ride The 'Uh Oh' Wave

When many employees get halfway to the end of the month and the 'uh oh' effect kicks in there are a few things that can happen especially if they are working towards sales or production targets. From an emotioneering perspective, the fear of not hitting goals or the worry of how to get there can start to set in. This can cause employees to cut corners or cause them to use pushy techniques that could lead to more complaints and affect their ability to get there. They may start to lose belief in themselves.

From a high performer's perspective, they could lose momentum after the halfway mark as they may feel extremely confident that they will achieve and lose a little motivation to keep going. The halfway mark is a clear point that will give an opportunity to realign, support and encourage the team to remain focused on the consistent behaviours that will bring about the results and how far they have to go.

> A surge of activity always came after the temporal midpoint 31

Emotioneering It

- Schedule the sessions in advance so they are not a big surprise to your team members.

- Ask them open questions about how they feel their month has started

- Share with them their performance metrics so far or ask them to talk about their performance so far.

- Go over the notes and action points agreed in the goal-setting session and update the progress. Discuss what has held them back from doing 'XYZ' if they haven't been met or celebrate if all are on the right track.

- Remind them of their overall motivation and finish with an uplifting message.

Namaste In The Game

♥

Running competitions for the team is one of my favourite things to put in place. The fun we have had over the years from some of the funniest games. They don't even have to cost much money outside of the budget. I remember interviewing a guy called Andy who used to work for a well-known mobile phone company who proceeded to tell me that he had the highest performing teams in the UK and all he did was have a shield that he passed around the team every month depending on who was top of the leader board and that's all they would get, the pride to have it and the person who had it the most over the year got to keep it. Simple yet extremely effective.

One of the best ones that I have created for a client was during the times of the 'ice bucket challenge'. The UK director, the UK Head of Operations and I, as their Performance Consultant decided to create a competition where for every 5 x upgrades the sales team achieved. They could nominate a bucket of water to be poured over one of the three of us. This was a UK wide competition run over a weekend, so there were many teams. Once the competition was over each of us had to record a video with the water being poured over us for each team's nominated bucket.

I will never forget the delight on my now husbands face when I told him he could pour 4 buckets of cold water over me, I just wish he hadn't gone so slow! The video also included me shouting and shrieking to ask him to speed up – much to the team's delight! The same could be said for the other two videos, great fun, something very memorable, lifted the spirits whilst bringing in a record-breaking sales weekend. I would do it again in a heartbeat.

Reach New Heights

Starting something new or doing something that has never been done before can be quite a challenge. There is a lot to focus on in the workplace and after an initial period of working in a certain role, it can become habitual. When something becomes habitual there is a reduction of dopamine which is the reward-seeking hormone so the initial buzz that once was there has subsided and now things are in much more of a routine. Whilst this can also cause people to start to think about new hobbies or adventures it could also lead them to start to look outside the company for a new role.

That being said people also like to stick to what they know 'in the comfort zone' so if they have been selling a certain product or service for a while then it can become second nature to them so when you bring in a new product or service there is no immediate benefit to them as individuals then you could wonder why this product or service isn't doing as well as you would have hoped when they simply aren't presenting it. On the flip side, the comfort zone could also lead those unmotivated team members to stay and become more bored and negative towards their role. So, it really is a double edge sword. Competitions and games bring about the dopamine rush and fun that many employees love. They support behaviour change, new possibilities in terms of metrics and help us to retain new knowledge through learning.

87% of employees agree gamification makes them more productive [32]

Emotioneering It

- Run competitions at least once per month.
- Make it fair. For example, if you are going to do it just based on revenue then ask yourself if it will demotivate many of the team
- Run the competition over a short period of time. Don't lose the excitement by making the end goal too far away.
- Ensure it engages as many of the team as possible. The aim is to involve your team and improve relationships.
- Align the competition with a business objective. Whether that is relationship building or promoting a new product or service.
- The prize doesn't have to be costly to the business although if the potential return of investment is a big one, then why not?!
- Make sure people know how to play and how they can win clearly.

Who Needs A Hero?

Have you ever worked somewhere and there is a certain person that people would secretly prefer never take annual leave because what would everyone do without them? They are the go-to person, the lifeline in the team and if something goes wrong, they are the first person to call, as a firefighter. These are the heroes. The challenge with having a hero in the team is that it shows there are inefficiencies, gaps in skill and not enough knowledge shared between people.

The hero might take a big ego boost from all this before getting to the point that they can no longer work at this rate before burnout. If this is the case then it is time to get more people involved, define processes, or create new ones. I was recently talking to a great person, and they introduced me to the term 'Hackathon' this is very common in the tech world where at least two groups of developers would spend a weekend or a few days attempting to come up with the finished solution and the event would be gamified.

Collaboration is really the key to continuous improvement. Stay green and continue to grow by encouraging brainstorming and the hackathon concept. I highly suggest, for further reading, the book How to Succeed with Continuous Improvement by Joakim Ahlstrom.

Hackathons & Brainstorms

In a dynamic fast-moving world continuous improvement is crucial to survival and adding a competitive edge within the business. According to Mckinsey 96% of executives have factored innovation into their business strategy and expressed its importance. So, what is actually being done to foster it? You will also hear many employees say 'I'm just not that creative' when in fact they have lost a lot of the ability to bring creativity into their life. We are all born creative, and we lose a lot of it over time. Often our emotions and interpretations can get in the way for example 'I'm an adult, I'm not playing that childish game' or thoughts of 'what if I come out with a stupid idea'. So, we can stay silent and choose not to participate.

I interviewed Phil Tottman co-founder of Book of Beasties, and they are very centred around wellness for children. He told me that he and the co-founder came up with Fridea – That Fridays were for creativity and play. I love it! The impact of bringing more innovation to the workplace can promote person-based thinking through a humanistic approach and it builds empathy through simulation of different scenarios even if in augmented reality. We feel it even though we are not in it.

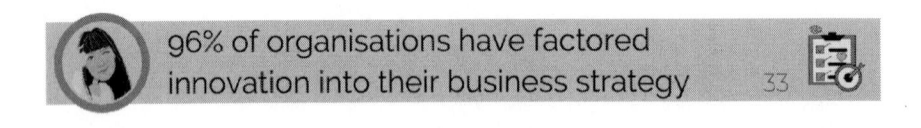

> 96% of organisations have factored innovation into their business strategy 33

Emotioneering It

- Always be open to suggestions. Encourage ideas and suggestions as much as possible.
- Make white space or time for creativity in the schedule. Ask your team to do a time audit over a week to know what they are doing and focusing on. To see what can be moved or lowered in priority.

- Take up something new. Things that encourage a different thought pattern and will increase creativity are arts and crafts, musical instruments, language, writing, meditation, roleplay in the form of improvision.

- Look at the relationships in the team. Are certain people cutting others off mid-sentence, or dismissing their ideas totally? Encourage the dialogue 'yes and...' instead of 'yes but...'.

- Reduce stress and anxiousness as much as possible by increasing the production of oxytocin and serotonin as these promote cell generation and growth. This will also help you stay in the present moment to focus on the mind.

Five

Culture

♥

The DNA of a Company

There are a lot of people that talk about culture and how to shape the culture of a company. Essentially it comes down to one thing –

Culture is the DNA of a company.

It's the identity, life, soul and heartbeat of a team or organisation. It's who you are as a group. It's contributed to by everything the collective does. It starts and ends with the core values and how these are part of the day to day. Interwoven into the way you communicate and the way these spill over into how the team FEEL about it. It's the story. The losses and the wins. It's how the journey has been navigated so far. Ask yourself how you would describe the culture at your company, write it down, then ask the team how they would describe it. Would there be a theme song? A set of commandments? Would what you wrote down and what the team said match?

Not too long ago I worked with a car rental team at Heathrow. They were strong in terms of performance and had a lot of heart although Casey, the Station leader at the time, and I, felt something was missing. Something that could bind them like a sense of identity. I was working with them as a Senior Performance Consultant. We discussed it and decided to come up with a team name. There was a competition to come up with a name and not before long 'The Heathrow Hurricanes' were born. It didn't stop there the name started to take on a life of it's own being interwoven in to all areas of operations.

For example, they started an employee of the month called 'The Eye of The Storm', there were 10 hurricane commandments created, a news board called the Weather Station, and a daily team brief called the Tailwind. Now all this sounds fun right or cheesy depending on which way you look at it and you might be sceptical about whether it even made a difference.

The thing is they started to have their own language, experience and things that were unique to them as a team which increased their sense of pride, comradery, and engagement. The performance that followed in terms of service and sales results increased by another 20% on top of already outstanding numbers. Now that was something to see and I will never forget the Hurricane DNA.

There are so many ways that you can build a strong team culture and part of that is to create unique experiences for the team as much as possible. These don't have to cost money although investing in your people is important.

EMOTIONEERING BUSINESS RESULTS

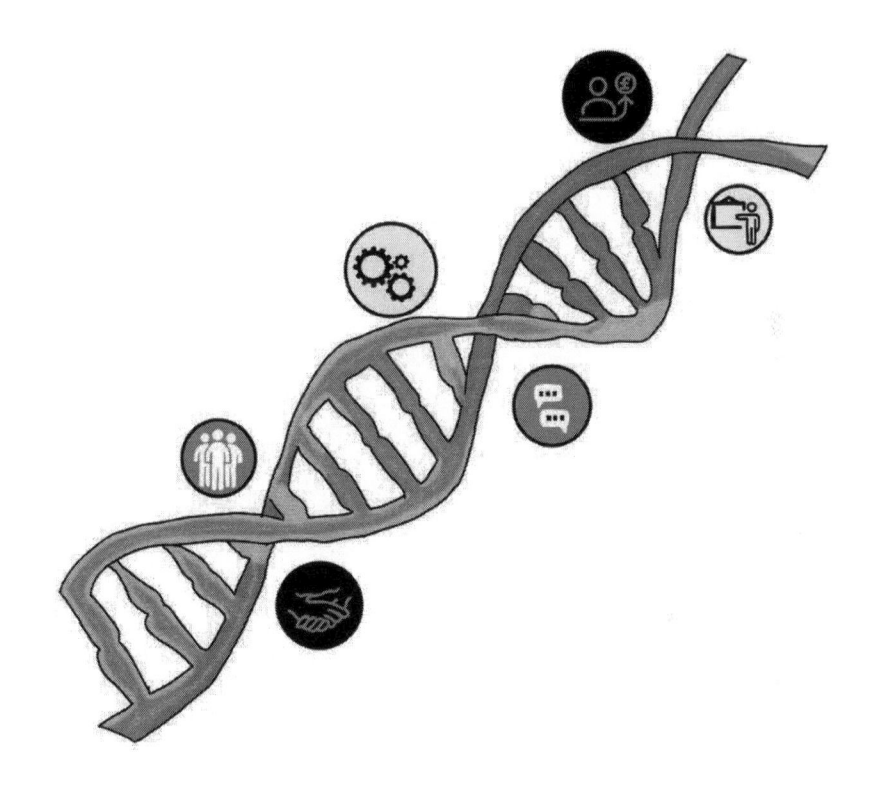

Vision

♥

Do you dare to dream bigger? Do you see things others will say is impossible? I am one of those people that firmly believe where there is a will there is a way. I was working with an automotive firm that had a sister company in the group that was low cost and unfortunately was considered the not so hot version of what was offered. I have always believed that regardless of whether something is low cost or not the one fundamental thing that matters is the customer interaction with the employees on the frontline. Having deeply studied both brands, I believed that the low-cost brand could triple its results and rival the current performance of the premium brand, without cutting corners, by implementing the full framework and delivering a great service. It took some time, of course, it did, nothing great was ever built overnight, although I think that what made it even sweeter was that 1 year into the project that is what happened...

The largest flagship location of each brand were within fractions of each other and the low-cost sister company had tripled performance. You should have seen the faces of the senior team that worked across both brands. Both feelings of shock and elation. Some disbelieving that it was being done correctly although upon site visits and their own internal investigation found it all to be fascinating and helped them take new motivation back to the premium brand to aim for the stars. The premium brand, from the learnings, then increased by a third too. You've got to love an underdog story! To all the low-cost brands with, unique offerings and brilliant service, I salute you. Look at Netflix, Spotify and many more. The differentiator? Vision.

Influence The Dream To Reality

The unwavering belief and vision that a leader must have to drive an organisation forward are hard to come by. The mentality of 'there has to be a better way' is in short supply. Of course, vision does come with its own challenges because when you have it, it's then about being able to articulate it and communicate it in a way that others really understand what you are looking for. The big challenge for visionaries is that other people often find it hard to believe that what you propose is possible so your level of influence to bring a dream to reality must be a strong skill. Vision without action is only a dream. Getting a team to believe and be passionate about it enough to drive the action with you and for the greater good is tough.

The other side of vision is that living with your mind in the future can be an anxious place to be, mix this with impatience to see it become a reality and it can be a mix of emotions that are hard to manage. It could lead to missing an opportunity to appreciate the process or the small milestones along the way. Having self-awareness through emotional intelligence is critical. Also having a strong vision doesn't mean that every idea is a winner and being able to set aside the emotion to think rationally becomes key. Ever heard the phrase 'don't kick the baby!'? Becoming extremely attached to ideas can really challenge a leader to be able to look at the cold hard facts about a business.

Whilst this may put a cautious view on vision, I will say that to lead an organisation it is crucial to its success. It just comes with some pitfalls to be mindful of.

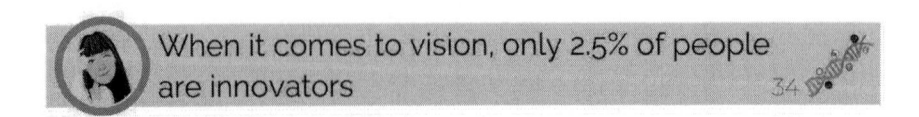

> When it comes to vision, only 2.5% of people are innovators
>
> 34

Emotioneering It

- Dream bigger. Whilst I spoke about not every idea becoming a reality do not let this deter you. Do not let anyone dampen your dreams of a better future. Find a way to make it work within business. If you want record-breaking results and better team performance through being able to change the world for your customers and team then go for it.

- You are allowed. Let's silence the inner voice that may be saying things like, 'who do you think you are?', 'what am I thinking? or 'who am I to be doing or thinking this?'. To silence it first we must recognise it. Then reframe everything you are saying into a new affirmation for example 'all great things started with the idea of just one person' or 'You are worthy of doing this just as much as anyone else that has gone before you'. Other people will try and stifle your dreams and visions you may just find your worst enemy is yourself though. Your internal self-image is far more important in helping you achieve new greater levels of results.

- Take some reflection time as a leader and work out what a 10 out of 10 day in your life would look like and feel like for you. Write down all the details. Then work out how to close the gap. (if you are already living your 10 out of 10 days then go you! Now let's help others get there)

Mission Statement

♥

In 2015 there was breaking news on the biggest deception to ever happen in the automotive industry. The largest car manufacturer in history had been cheating vehicle emissions and this had been for six years. Think of the thousands, if not millions of customers that had unknowingly bought one of their cars now feeling deceived. Let me point out, the stock nosedived by 40%. The CEO resigned and as much as they lost revenue it was the damage to the reputation which was even more costly. How could this have happened? Senior leaders in the race to be the best and beat Tesla to the top mark had cut corners and cheated the system. A collection of decisions that ultimately led to their downfall. Their mission that was delivered to the shareholders was "The main goal of the group's strategy is for Volkswagen to become the economic and ecological leader of the global automotive industry"

Well, the decision had made them look the most ecological on paper when in reality they were not. They ultimately wanted to beat the competition and be number one at all costs. Detailing in the objective that they wanted to achieve this by 2018. This race had now lost them billions. I'm sure a collection of decisions that they will never make again. The difference between Tesla and Volkswagen was that they had a purpose, the had vision that led them to make choices based on making decisions for the good of mankind. Elon Musk had realised if you ask smart and accurate questions, the solutions would present themselves. His question, inspired by Einstein about asking the right questions, was 'what things will have a great impact on the future of humanity's destiny?'.

The impact of a mission statement goes far beyond the year that it is written or the paper it is written on. I was extremely particular about the mission of the Modern Mind Group.

> We are emotioneering to change the hearts and minds of at least one million people for the better.

To make an impactful difference to peoples lives in and out of the corporate world.

We've only just scratched the surface.

It's the Umbrella Of Everything You Do As A Business

In a business, the mission statement really sets you apart and can keep employees motivated on the journey with you. Without it, the company will lack direction and decisions are made with a different intention, which impacts innovation and the way that the team work together. A challenge can be that the leader doesn't know how to set a mission statement or could be saying things to themselves like 'who am I to be setting this goal?' or 'Are we good enough to do that?' As I mentioned in the last chapter. It's all linked. These thoughts come from a lack of belief and that negative bias or inner critic again can creep in because a mission statement is bold and sets you apart. Moving away from the herd and starting to differentiate yourself is an emotioneering process.

Remember, the strongest trees and plants aren't grown in the forest protected from the elements, they are grown, often alone, in the strongest winds. Finding the time to reflect on the mission and what is the overall goal may take some time and deep thought. There are also many tools to help you. A mission statement is an umbrella to everything else you do as a business. Don't delay and start to create this today.

If you are a company with one already, the challenge will be educating everyone else on it, making sure it is part of induction plans and part of daily communication. Can it be seen? Do the team know it? Do they live by it?

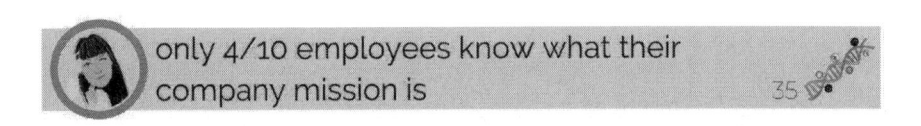

> only 4/10 employees know what their company mission is 35

Emotioneering It

If you have a mission statement,

- Ask yourself if it is inspiring and still fit for purpose? Then if so, know it off by heart and ensure you can share it with the team.

- Assess if people know the mission statement and educate them on it. So that decisions and objectives come back to it every time.

If you don't have a mission statement

- Go back to the roots. Who is the person that created the company or group of people? Why did they decide to start it? What difference were they aiming to make?

- Decide if you want to make a finite mission statement or an infinite one

- Take some time to reflect on what the objectives are as well as the values. Think about what the vision is for 10 – 20 years from now

- Start to record what ideas come to your head. Don't worry if you feel like cringing at the first few, it's part of the process of getting to the right one for you and the team.

- Give yourself a date to ensure one is set. If you leave this open it will get pushed down the priority list.

MELISSA CURRAN

Values

♥

Across the world, in the southern hemisphere, there is a rugby team that no one even calls by their actual name. The New Zealand International Rugby Team are known as The All Blacks. A name they have acquired over many years, almost 120, and it has stuck. It's part of the brand and the culture of the team. This team has the highest winning record of any team at a 77.7% win rate. Are one of only 2 teams to win the Rugby World Cup 3 Times (the other being South Africa) and all from a country that is home to less than 5 million people. Phenomenal! As a Welsh woman and rugby fan, it pains me slightly to talk about this in here, maybe I should have spoken about the 6 Nations Tournament, although the best are the best for a reason. Ha! It's all fair in love and rugby, right?! So, what makes them different?

The All Blacks have mastered the art of core team values. A set of 15 principles in fact, that bring them collaboration, coordination, comradery, and celebration. Let me give you a flavour of them. 'Write your legacy', when any new player joins the team, they are given a book which contains pictures of the shirts that have played before them as well as blank pages for the future, this shows that there is history still to be made.

Another one I truly love is "sweep the sheds", this is about remembering humility, setting aside ego and remembering that no matter who we are we are never too good to clean our own changing room. "From the very start, you learn humility. There are these structures in place, like the fact that we always leave the changing room as clean as when we walked in. So, you'll often see Richie McGaw and the coach Steve Hansen sweeping the shed" said Dan Carter, International Professional All Blacks Rugby Player and legend of the sport. The impact of values is clear to see.

Values Drive Decisions

In a team where the values haven't been set, it can be a challenge to know where and how to start. The decisions and behaviours that the team displays can be very different to what is needed to move the company and brands towards the objectives set out from the corporate strategy. It also isn't about a copycat approach and becoming the next All blacks, Nike or Coca-Cola. This won't be lived and breathed the same as if they have been created together. That bond that I talked about at the start of the chapter won't be as strong without them. Think, 'what do we want?', 'what do we not tolerate?' and 'how do we want to be remembered?'.

For a company that set values at the beginning of the company, the challenge could be that 1) no one knows them and maybe they don't even know they exist 2) The values may have been right for the original strategy and now as the company has evolved, they don't sit right or need to be updated. 3) With an established team the challenge can also be in creating those values without their input, so they won't buy into them.

49% of employees don't' know their company values without looking for them 36

Emotioneering It

- If you already have company values that have been created. Quiz the team and see if they know them off by heart. If they don't ensure they are part of daily communication and somewhere they can see them. Think posters, stickers, banners, the top of meeting agendas and minutes. The aim is for them to be considered before each decision that is made. Set an expectation to know them and run a competition to speed up the learning process with gamification.

- If the company does not have them defined or the company has evolved so that they must now change, look at the results of the employee engagement survey and notice what the team are saying about their work and how they feel about it. Look for common themes.

- Then tell the team that you want to create the values together. Educate them on what values are. For example, you could get them to read this chapter to first understand and then ask them to come up with 5 each (some will overlap and may be similar). From that assign a maximum of 10 values for the company. Then communicate and follow point 1.

The Ministry of Fun

♥

One of my first ever jobs was working for a company called Admiral Car Insurance. It was a company started by Henry Englehart and I remember the first time I met him after all these years. He handed me a jigsaw piece as well as everyone else and said never forget that without you this can't be a masterpiece. Very inspiring. He genuinely cared about the people.

One of the initiatives that Admiral had was that they appointed a Ministry of Fun for each department and this for our department was Rebecca. She had all the energy and enthusiasm for it. She would organise fun days and activities that could be outside or inside the office. One day I arrived to work, and Rebecca said right "MM10 you're on the list for crazy office golf at 2pm." MM10, DK3, JM10 and many others were our work system codes and also made up part of the culture. That internal language made us part of Admiral that no one else outside the team understood. The unique experience.

Anyway, sure enough at 2pm, I went to see what was going on around the corner of the office and someone had constructed an obstacle course for crazy golf overnight. It wasn't even work-related it was just something to lift our spirits and a break from the norm of the day-to-day call centre. The Admiral Group to this day still has a strong culture and many of their employees are shareholders in the company.

Moodhovers Suck

The work environment can become quite monotonous. Creating an environment that encourages people to smile, have fun and lift their spirits often takes more than the norm. In many locations across the globe, there are event calendars that increase tourism, bookings, footfall and in turn sales.

Running a fun day or themed day even on your busiest days can help to keep customers entertained and in a good mood even at the sight of a slightly longer queue as well as lifting the spirits of your team. It often doesn't take much or cost much to do this and have everyone smiling.

If you are a virtual team, you may think this section is not relevant, I bet the majority of your team think differently and would love to get involved in something. Ask them for ideas on how to make it happen and the solutions will often present themselves.

Customers that have to queue for services or to speak to someone can find it quite tedious. Having a themed day can break it up a little and help the wait to seem a little less painful. Ever wondered why those theme parks have long snaking queues that are interactive? They have to entertain people for hours.

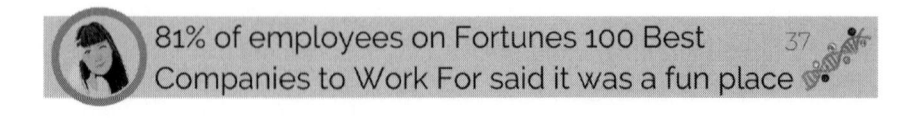

> 81% of employees on Fortunes 100 Best Companies to Work For said it was a fun place 37

Emotioneering It

A strong recommendation would be to ensure that one fun day would happen per month.

- Gain buy into the initiative from your leadership team through the influence that this is a great initiative that will increase results and engagement

- Look at the annual events calendar for the year. For example – Formula One at Silverstone or Notting Hill Carnival. If there is a month where nothing is particularly planned ask the team to come up with ideas for themes –for example, a charity bake-off and all made cakes for example or had a buffet – you can get as creative as you like.

- Now that the dates and themes have been chosen, let's get them communicated. People can then plan and start to get excited.

- Then when the time comes decorate, or apply the theme, costumes, banners or and props etc. If it is a remote team. Get creative with pictures, email signatures, zoom calls, themed email communication etc.

- Designate someone responsible for taking pictures and videos to be able to share afterwards or keep as team memories. You could even involve clients or customers if it is appropriate.

Let The Light In

♥

You may have heard episode 62 of the Emotioneering podcast with Mark Drager. It was probably some of the most fun I've had interviewing someone so far and it all started because he said the phrase "Oh, I'm sorry, is this a serious podcast?" ha! He is electric and the energy just bounced off each other. I highly suggest you check it out. The thing is there are some people that we work with that bring in the light and the fun. They are like sunshine on a cloudy day.

There have been many workplaces where I have worked, and we just had the best time. The work got done with high performance although people were able to enjoy themselves. Mahreen, Alex and Cosmina were people where we knew there would be fun that day and I looked forward to my client visits with them. Then there were other teams or client locations that I would visit where everyone including the manager were just miserable, not one smile, not one laugh. My aim would be to attempt to lift the mood and bring positivity although it wasn't always reciprocated. This is when you know there is something that is broken and the team spirit is absent.

Have you ever heard "oh that's just what they are like in 'xyz'" or "It's always been like that in 'abc'. Well, I find it hard to accept that it is ok to have a team in an environment where nothing grows. When you give negative energy to sunflowers they wilt and die. Give them light and positivity and they will flourish. When plants don't grow we change the environment not the plants. One of the other great guests that I had on the podcast was Kev Orkian, head of Jongelurs well known Comedy and Entertainment in the UK. Laughing is good for the soul.

Laughter and Productivity Can Coexist

There are still people out there that think that laughter indicates that no work is being done. Work is where we spend a lot of our time and laughter is a cure for a lot of the challenging times that life can throw at us. People connect and build stronger relationships with those that can lift spirits and bring positive energy.

Often, we can get so driven into the day to day that as leaders we can often neglect to check the pulse and ensure the team feels good. Fun and laughter is like someone opening the blinds and letting the light in. There are much more possibilities and I've seen people be more energised by this. Take a moment to stop and observe your team. How much laughter and fun can you hear? Are people enjoying their work environment?

> The average adult laughs 17 times per day versus 300 as a child

Emotioneering It

- Take some time to understand how the ego works. When it comes to the ability to laugh and not take ourselves too seriously it is often inhibited by our ego. Everyone has an ego. We often think of it in a way that is associated with people who are loud and expressive, for example, a rockstar, when this is not the case. We all have an ego. The more we recognise it the more we can keep it under control the better our humour will be.

- Set aside 5 minutes to find a quick and funny video related to the job you all do and share it with your team. I understand that not everyone has the same humour although they will appreciate the gesture if the tone is right.

- Being a leader that can make others laugh or bring joy to the workplace is actually something you can learn. I suggest checking out the Emotioneering Podcast episode 43. Emotioneering Expression Through Comedy and episode 44. Which is my interview with Kev Orkian CEO of Jongleurs, The largest comedy club in the UK. It is a skill you can master and increases your charisma as a leader.

- No one is expecting you as a leader to become a stand-up comedian, it's about lightening the mood for your team and helping make it a fun place to be. We spend more time at work than anywhere else.

Out Of The Workplace

♥

There have been many times over the years that I have attended work trips or team activities away from the workplace. They are great bonding experiences for the team which build comradery, trust and moments that are unique memories that often last a lifetime. One fond memory that springs to mind is when a team I worked with went on a planned trip to Scotland and there was a new consultant called Ben who had joined the team although no one had really met him before. Fast forward a few hours later following dinner and one of the activities was for us all to re-enact Lip Sync Battle. Where you pick a song, mouth the words to the music and get voted on performance. Everyone and I mean everyone in the team participated, when it was the new guy Ben's turn though, his rendition of Taylor Swift's, Shake it Off, wiped the floor with everyone else's and he was a hands-down winner. Lots of fun and something that all of us will remember.

Meet Up Magic

Remote teams, different shift patterns, some team members engaged and some members not, makes the thought of attempting to get everyone together a little overwhelming. The reality is that it is highly unlikely that you are going to please everyone so even offering an out of work activity or meet up means a lot to most of the team. Another challenge can be when it comes to budget. It does not have to cost a lot some teams I know went for a long scenic walk or picnic (bring your own food and drinks).

It is really about the experiences and memories that are being created. It allows teammates the chance to relate to each other in a different way and see each other as individuals with passions, hobbies, likes and dislikes. I understand that 2020 put a stop to those that had planned in these types of face-to-face activities, for a little while so I encourage you to think 'so what is possible instead?' 'what is the way around this?' Where there is a will there is a way.

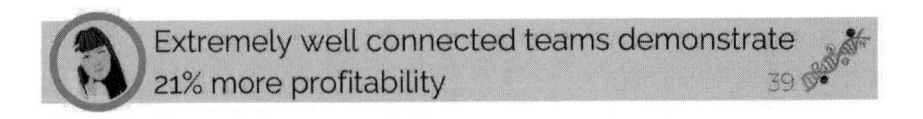

> Extremely well connected teams demonstrate 21% more profitability 39

Emotioneering It

- Ensure that there is a meet up at least once per quarter
- Get the team involved in what they would like to do
- Remember it does not need to cost a lot or even anything at all. It is about the experience and the time spent together.
- Aim to get as many of the team involved as possible, with shift patterns this may be a challenge for 100% of the team to be there. Consider whether other teams could cover for yours and then your team could return the favour if the challenge is about shifts and locations.

♥ · ♥ · ♥ · ♥ · ♥

The Number One Reason People Don't Open Up

♥

People go through many moments in their life that can be quite traumatic. Losing a loved one, going through a divorce, financial challenges. These can affect our physical, mental and social wellbeing. Essentially health is a triangle of these three points and when these are all in a good state then our life fulfilment is likely to be better too. After losing my dad I started to experience anxiety on planes, full-on panic attacks every time I would fly. Sometimes they would happen even with the thought of having to fly the next day. I kept a lot of this to myself, although after speaking to a good friend and colleague they suggested I speak to someone and get some professional help to see if this could resolve the panic attacks and anxiety. This started me on a journey of deeper self-discovery and helped me to develop a toolkit for flying, as well as reducing my anxiety.

What I also learned from that was that I wasn't in the best position to help someone else in the workplace if they were also suffering. I decided to become a counsellor after the sessions myself so that I could really understand how to ask better questions, hold space for someone, be less dismissive of their feelings and reserve judgement. When a person is not physically well, we often know what to say or how to help although when it is mental wellbeing that is the cause of distress, many people don't know what to say. In 2008 BMC health services did a study on users or patients of a hospital for mental illness. This was the first-ever study that was done on the patients, the people receiving the treatment and what they found from the study was that 100% of them mentioned trust in the understanding of them getting better. Trust is the number one reason people don't open up and this affects a person's mental state of mind.

It's Not The Cherry On Top

Many companies and business leaders will approach wellbeing as a project or one-off initiative. For wellbeing to be taken seriously, for mental and physical health, it has to become part of the business day today. BAU (Business as Usual) vs a project. Projects or one off initiatives aren't always taken seriously and feel to the team like you could be putting a plaster over something rather than addressing the real issues. Another barrier can be that we often fear what we don't understand so a lack of training on mental health or wellbeing can cause any initiatives to be avoided.

Something else that can happen is that companies will move away from performance focus not wanting to 'apply stress' when in fact goal setting, conversations about abilities and skillsets can, when feedback is delivered correctly, cause positive stress. This positive stress can lead to a sense of pride and achievement, from doing a great job or contributing to the team.

A remote or hybrid workplace also presents new challenges on wellbeing. This is where strong relationships and non-objective meetings are key. Without trust and strong communication, a leader will not be able to see the whole picture and will be basing their understanding on assumptions. A lack of appropriate questions won't reveal the information required to get a better understanding. Seek to understand.

Another challenge can also be toxic positivity in the workplace. Morgan Clements recently wrote about this on our Modern Mind Group Blog. For example, using phrases such as "everything happens for a reason" or "Think happy thoughts" can leave a person feeling that their emotions are being swept aside and not addressed. The only way to keep a team positive and optimistic is to listen to them, support them and give them hope rather than by using dismissive statements. This isn't often intentional, it's because the leader making these statements doesn't know that they are dissmissive or hasn't been taught alternative dialogues. Try "I'm glad you are talking to me about it." Or "Your feelings make sense and are normal, what can I do to support you with this?". These will have more impact and help your team to open up to you.

Some companies now realise that sometimes not feeling great mentally is part of being human, choosing to adopt duvet days or reflection days as part of their long-term initiatives.

Wellbeing affects absence rates or through presenteeism, where an employee does not take time off, it can be extremely damaging to their health.

> 32% of people have felt lonely in the workplace 40

Emotioneering It

There is so much that can be done here although as mentioned the aim is to make something part of what you do that sits within the culture of the business. The first way to ensure that it becomes a focus is to educate and inform.

- Ensure everyone in the team has access to a mental health awareness course. Not an extremely short 30-minute eLearning one that is a tick box exercise. A course that has an impact will typically last a day with an assessment to check they understand.
- Choose mental health and wellbeing champions to run periodic initiatives for the team. Talks on different subjects for awareness, for example, addiction, domestic violence, mindset, financial understanding, diversity and inclusion as well as many more. I recently worked with a private school in Cardiff. Their morality and

wellbeing coordinator Cathryn Annwyl-Williams does a fantastic job at arranging these initiatives for the students and teachers alike.

- Ensure leaders are focusing on their relationships with the team to build trust so that they can be open about how they feel.

- Help leaders in your team improve their questioning and listening skills to encourage dialogue from their team.

- Wellbeing groups around nutrition and fitness to encourage participation. For example, the 'mountain step challenge', a number of steps per day or charity fun run.

- Observe the language the team are using and be aware of toxic positivity statements. Share best practices on what to say instead when team members are expressing their feelings.

- Provide an EAP (employee assistance programme) many of these initiatives that companies offer can help employees with their mental health, finances, family challenges, bereavement, occupational or physical therapy. Then encourage the team to use it and get familiar with the process of using this benefit.

- The Mindset Score – this is a resource that we offer which is a scorecard that can track how your team feel monthly to educate them and give you as a leader an overview of the company mindset overall. This would be anonymous at an organisational level to keep the mindset score private and confidential for the team members. Get in touch with us at The Modern Mind Group to learn more. info@modernmindgroup.co.uk

· ♥ · ♥ · ♥ · ♥ · ♥ ·

Seeing is Believing

♥

I was visiting many different countries and field locations for a global brand. One of the major locations on the network was similar in size of business to that of a major UK one that was breaking records in terms of best practice, highest levels of implementation of the framework, highest revenue, lower customer complaints, fantastic culture/engagement and a leadership team that was loved by the employees. This was not the case for the other location. It was doing just over a third of the results. After visiting both, I believed it was possible for this lower-performing location to at least double its results.

I worked with an amazing consultant and asked her what she thought the challenge was. She told me that the management team at the time had team calls and heard what was possible but didn't really believe it. We devised a plan together for a site visit for her and the champion to visit the UK location over two days. We thought if they could just see it with their own eyes, assess it and experience it, that their belief would go up as well as open them up to the possibilities.

So that's what we did. After her great influence and proposal of the idea to the senior client team, she and the location manager visited the UK location. It improved their relationship as well as doing exactly what we thought it would. Fast forward to only 12 weeks later.... On the busiest month of the year for the business. This location doubled its results seeing another half a million in revenue in just one month (not a bad return for a few hundred pounds 2-day trip). We celebrated on a call together and the best bit she said was that the culture had started to really change and there was still more to come. Opportunity rocks!

Best Practice Shared

Imagine what would happen if everyone in my volleyball team just started to do their own thing? With no coordination, no trust in the other person's abilities and no appreciation for the best-in-class examples of spikes, bumps, or volleys? It would lead to lost games, a lack of competitive edge and an unhappy team not to mention an unfulfilled coach.

In the business especially when you have multiple locations working in isolation this can lead to so much untapped potential. From an emotioneering point of view the team will make excuses by blaming things on customers, the weather anything that points away from them now understanding how to make things work or they may have a lack of belief that is possible as they have never seen it. Really being able to share the best-in-class lessons with your team and defining excellence can show what is possible. These are perception gaps and there are four of them, overestimating performance, underestimating performance, overestimating the ability to be coached or underestimating their ability to change. Sharing best practices will give a leader something to benchmark when coaching to these perception gaps.

Many leaders could think that defining best practices is extremely time-consuming although the benefits far outweigh the investment of time.

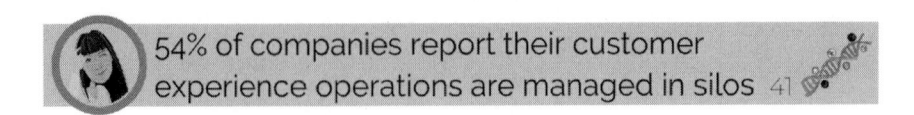

54% of companies report their customer experience operations are managed in silos 41

Emotioneering It

- Make a list of the tasks and procedures people have to do within their roles

- Ask whether standard operation procedures (SOPs) exist for all of the activities that the company does. If yes, then check them and ensure they are up to date. If not, then start a project to work through them and get them created over a certain time frame i.e. 3 – 6 months. The larger the company the bigger this task will be.

- Look at each SOP and decide who has created the BEST-in-class example for that procedure. Can it be shared in the form of audio, documentation of communication, a video or step by step guide?

- Communicate these with the team as part of your LMS, shared services drive or intranet. They need to be somewhere accessible for people.

- Have group meetings or conference calls where you ask certain leaders/people to share presentations, stories and results from new initiatives or projects that they have been running to make others aware of the possibilities.

- As you come across great examples of excellence or best practice, make notes, take pictures or record with the person's permission to collate share or update old versions.

- Inspect what you expect – whether you call it assessing, auditing or grading it is important to know whether the procedures are being followed. There may be performance gaps to close or high performance to shout about. Benchmarks can then be worked towards.

- As I suggested in the story if you have best operating practices that demonstrate operational excellence can you help other leaders in the team to realise what is possible by arranging site visits? Seeing is believing.

Ethics & Social Commitment

♥

In 2020 my brother and I with a passion for paddleboarding co-founded SUP Wales. We saw an opportunity where other groups were not providing enough information or promoting safety techniques to support the growing paddleboarding community, so we decided to create one. It has grown and there is now a Facebook community of close to 8,000 members. There is also a partner programme and my brother, Julian is contacted frequently with merchandise and products to promote to the community.

The challenge is that many of these products don't match SUP Wales ethics or corporate responsibility policy. Sustainability and social responsibility is a hot topic for many governments and in Wales, this is being advocated strongly especially for new businesses and start-ups. To Julian and I, if it means at times turning down partnerships because of that then so be it. It's about the community and people want to know what you stand for.

Live By the Social Sword You Are Swinging

A company without a Corporate Social Responsibility policy can limit its appeal when being chosen by other companies to partner with as well as candidates choosing to work with your organisation over another.

For an established business the emotioneering side of corporate social responsibility when one did not previously exist could be that if they really want to do good in the world then it can't just be a written document, it has to be something that the company stands by, always. That means that some of the companies or partnerships a company already has could be in direct conflict with the CSR. This could mean losing some clients or having tough conversations about how they plan to adapt in that area so that the partnership can continue. Not every business leader is prepared to stop working with certain partnerships if the newly defined standards do not meet the expectations. This of course can be viewed as a short-term loss for a long-term gain although it can become complicated.

For a new business, the emotioneering side could be the fear of losing work because of it or having to turn down new business due to the CSR. In the modern world, the CSR can really add to your brand story and many new partnerships start with aligning on ethics so on the positive side it can increase your attractiveness, get you great press relations for a competitive edge and make you very appealing for new recruits in the job market. Governments are also encouraging new businesses to put their sustainability policies in place now to ensure that the environment is looked after for years to come.

From an employee perspective without a CSR they can find it hard to find purpose or feel engaged with the business objectives. Part of fulfilment in our lives as humans are the feelings we get from doing good for others and society. A strong CSR will give them something to shout about as a brand ambassador and also a sense of pride about the company they work for.

79% of people would decline a job offer due to unethical standards   42

Emotioneering it

- Look at the companies' values as well as the core competencies. Start there. For example, for a company that has the value of 'helping people achieve regardless of their background or skillset' a company could choose something like funding 2 scholarships for the year to a college programme. For a company that has the value of 'ensuring the environment is better with our impact' it could be keeping corporate flights to a minimal level per year or making a pledge to only use recycled products and furniture or having a cycle to work scheme. These are examples of changes although the bolder the better.

- Be willing to turn down work and opportunities to ensure that you uphold the CSR. 87% of consumers on a recent survey by Cone Communications CSR Study, said they would be more likely to purchase from a company that has a social or environmental policy that aligned with what they cared about. It's not about what you repel, it's what you attract.

- Ensure the team know about it and can be involved with supporting the initiatives. They must be initiatives that help the team feel proud to work where they do.

Standards of Excellence

♥

When I was growing up, I was enthusiastic about sport and in athletics, was really keen on the high jump. I would spend hours and hours of my own time, out of lessons, practising. Setting up the bar, adjusting my approach, then going again and again. There were many times I knocked the bar off, although the elation of clearing a new height made all the failed attempts worth it. Never in the years that I trained for the high jump did I ever consider lowering the bar to make it easier? I'm sure if you spoke to Jessica Ennis-Hill, Olympic Gold and World Record Breaker (who I'm not comparing myself with by the way ha! Although what an incredible role model) and asked her the same about her high jump training, that she would say the same.

Don't Settle For The Average

When excellence is not defined and standards are low it will lead to poor communication, conflict, low work performance and unpredictable results. Without defining excellence, it can lead to an unmotivated team that are unsure of what to aim for. Yes, having high standards can mean adjustments or a level of rework although the feeling of accomplishment and achievement when they are met or exceeded will be even greater.

What can happen with team performance is also that leaders set the bar at the average and focus there instead of focusing on the top 25% of performers and promoting the possibilities with that. This can be due to focusing on a bell curve of performance which can influence leaders to believe that there will always be underperformers and average performers which is not the case. The bell curve of performance can be evened out when excellence is defined and leaders are coaching their people towards that. For example, imagine a championship football team, the manager would not expect everyone to be the striker although they would expect them to be exceptional for their role within the team.

If you have an academy of strikers, then the aim is for them all to be aiming to be exceptional. What I mean by this is if you have more than one person in the same role then this is what you would want to aim for.

Excellence can be defined in any workplace. It is not about having awards for IOS or the IEC. It is your version of what is currently being produced in each area and selecting the best in class. The following year the measurement can be improved as well as the year after that. Developing a culture of operational excellence internally and externally.

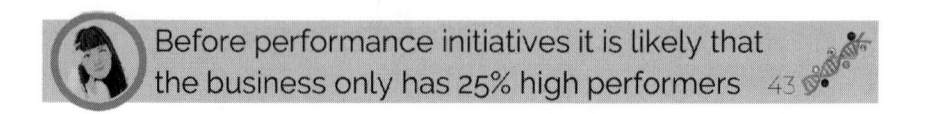

> Before performance initiatives it is likely that the business only has 25% high performers 43

Emotioneering It

- Look at the evidence across the team performance for metrics, competencies, attitudes and skills. Know what and who are the top 25%

- Look at the language and communication in the business, is it centred around the average performance or is it promoting a high standard? For example, 'as long as you are above the average' comments vs 'You deserve better and I want to help you get there, I believe in you'.

- Look at commission bands and do not have pay-outs that are below the average performance required for the collective team target. The team target will be the average, not the rule.

- Create an Elite club that the top 25% can be part of. For example, flight attendants receive a different colour or a gold badge for over a certain number of flights in their career. You want it to be a challenge to achieve the status and it shows others that there is something to strive towards and be recognised for.

- From setting standards of excellence and striving to do better for employees, society and customers look at what company awards can be applied for. You also deserve the accolades of getting to that level.

♥ ♥ ♥ ♥ ♥

Leadership

♥

There are many stories in history about how canaries were used in coal mines, to help the miners to know when it wasn't safe. Imagine this in a workplace setting and that the canaries are the employees. There are many people that ring in sick daily, due to depression or anxiety. People who suffer panic attacks are often suffering in silence and they don't tell anyone or are experiencing burnout, worrying that it will lead to losing their jobs. Reports indicate that 60% of sick leave is caused by stress. In some industries, this may be even higher. Over the years of delivering at pace, I too, experienced burnout. One thing I can say is, I wish I had been able to talk more openly with my line manager.

It is essentially down to trust and relationships. Train your managers to be better at being leaders of the people, or they are not the right person to be leading any team. Far too many people have been hurt by unskilled management. I hear things such as 'my boss doesn't have time for me' or 'I could never speak to my boss about that'. Well, canaries only sing when they are in good environments, they certainly weren't singing once they came out of those coal mines if there had been a toxic environment! I created the Canary Concept for this reason. 8 Key Factors to better leadership to create happier and healthier teams. These 8 Key Factors are communication, appreciation, notice, acceptance, relationships, imagination, empower and self-awareness. Let's do a deep dive into these.

Communication

Have you ever stopped to reflect on how you speak to your team and looked at the language that you use? Casey who I mentioned earlier in the book, is a business leader who in the early days of her career knew that she had to help her team improve their behaviours. One area was the practice element of the sales script and some of the language that Casey would use originally was for example "Can you practice your sales script for me today please?". Now on the face of it, there isn't anything particularly wrong with this language, it isn't unpolite, it's quite clear. What is an opportunity is the fact that this doesn't cover the impact of why it is important or play into what matters to that individual person. Casey would use similar language for many different aspects of the role.

Casey and I worked on how to adapt the conversation based on each individual and it had a much better impact on the team and the behaviour started to change sooner. The change based on this example was, "I highly encourage you to practice your sales script today when you do this Sarah, you are going to have much more flow which will build trust with your customers, getting you to that holiday you wanted much sooner, when will you schedule the time today?". Yes, it is a longer sentence. Yes, it takes more effort. Yes, it gets better results. Excellence is complex, not convenient.

Appreciation

The post landed on the mat and a small brown envelope was there with my name on it. As I opened it, I found a green piece of card with 9 positive character traits on there. How strange I thought. I turned it over to find my name on the back. With no explanation. Wow! I felt very valued, but where did it come from? A big smile came across my face and I felt very happy. I was on the phone to my line manager later that week and I told him about the story, he started to sound embarrassed and chuckled a little. He proceeded to tell me that the executive team had to submit a green card for a person in their team that they appreciated and put the character traits that made them great on it. He didn't tell me who it was from. I didn't really mind where it had come from. To receive recognition like this which was a small act of kindness is to this day one of the best things that have ever happened to me. So much so I still have it in a frame on my desk, ahead of other awards or certifications. This one green card reminds me of my value every single day. Thank you and Paul, I now know it was you.

Imagine being in a relationship with someone that never paid you any compliments, never gave thanks or showed appreciation, you probably wouldn't be with them for very long or it would cause so many arguments and conflicts. The thing is when it comes to our thoughts there are often a lot of good things in there the challenge is that our negative bias will always highlight the not so great points first. There is a brilliant TED talk by Chester Elton called Managing with Carrots. He has been dubbed the Apostle of Appreciation. Check it out and you will hear him reference the Harvard Business School study which concluded that a positive workplace has a ratio of 5:1 in terms of positive appreciative statements vs critical statements. Just because we are thinking it doesn't mean we are really saying or showing it. Great leaders look past the critical elements to find the positives first and that's how they deliver feedback.

Notice

There is a reason that a lifeguard will sit on a high tower above the pool and that the pool isn't unattended. I used to say to my team "I can't stop you from drowning if I don't know you are in the pool". A lifeguard can't simply wait in the back and be called when there is an emergency. Now that's also not saying that they are watching every single interaction that is happening in the pool at that time. They are looking to notice signs of distress. Flailing arms, lifelessness, or shouts. Then they are close by to respond quickly and appropriately.

There are three things here 1) are your team coming to you? 2) are you going to your team? 3) Do you notice when behaviour, attitude, or performance changes?

Acceptance

Wayne used to phone Sophie, his line manager, three or four times a day. Compared to the other employees in her team who would call her once or twice a week. Sophie saw four times a day as a complete inconvenience and had decided with her judgemental view that on the face of it, Wayne was incompetent. Rewind 6 months prior, Wayne worked for a very patient leader who knew he was competent although required a little more reassurance than the rest of his team. Sometimes Wayne's previous leader would answer, sometimes he wouldn't, although Wayne caused very few client complaints. The rest of the team loved him, and the customers did too. Both line managers had the same competent person only their acceptance of where Wayne was as a person was very different. They both also had an opportunity to help Wayne to grow and learn to be more self-assured in his actions and decisions. No leader ever gets a 'dream team' there are different personalities and different strengths. When we meet people where they are by accepting them and their journey, only then can we start to help them to change for their future benefit.

Relationships

"You're just not very fluffy," said the managing director of a company I worked for as a team manager, many years ago now. What they were trying to tell me was that whilst I had empathy and compassion, I was rarely showing these qualities at work. Well, on reflection whilst they were right about most of it, I was actually giving empathy and compassion to only those I had the strongest relationships with. Putting on the hard direct exterior that was often celebrated in business back then. Sound familiar?

Thankfully I learned from this feedback, increased my emotional intelligence, showed vulnerability, and built relationships through people first before the performance. The results that followed were incredible and many times record-breaking. I'm seeing the world start to change as the conversation about relationships being key in the workplace is taking more of a centre stage.

At the Modern Mind Group, Emotioneering and a people-first approach are rarely from our minds because we know how much of an impact it has on the wellbeing of the team as well as the results.

Harvard did a study on 'What Makes a Good Life?' it's the longest study to ever be conducted on adult development. The study had spanned over 75 years. They picked people for the study from many different backgrounds and what they found that makes a good life is the quality of your relationships. Not money, the house you live in, the job you have but the meaningful relationships you build up over time and those experiences that you share. They conclude that having meaningful relationships in life is one of the main motivational drivers of a human being.

I've been conducting leadership workshops and training for years. One of my favourite exercises is to ask the leaders whether they have a good relationship with their teams to which many people agree. Then I ask them to write down all of the names of the people in their team on the left-hand side of a piece of paper. Then I ask them to write down, next to each person, the month of their birthday, whether they have a partner or not, if so, what are their names, what car they drive (if so), what they are passionate about, what motivates them and what their favourite food is. Only 10% of any workshop I have ever delivered have been able to confidently complete 80% or more of the answers.

Imagination

"I don't know the answer" this is my brain at times, it isn't often although we are all human, so it happens. It's often at a time when I am in the thick of it, with work projects, consultancy delivery for clients and coordinating the team. I can have something come up that needs an answer, and, at that moment, I just don't have the capacity or energy for the thought process. However, when I am out running for my health some of the BEST ideas and solutions come to me. Why? Because of the white space. These gaps in the diary allow for activities away from the doing, the concentrating and the executing.

Nasa did a study to see the difference in creativity from being children to being adults. Nasa found that we are 96% less creative than we were as children. The main reasons are energy, process overload, leadership not factoring it in, people working in silos and fear of not wanting to express ideas or appear silly (for example may say "I'm an adult, I shouldn't be doing that").

Knowing this information, I aim to ensure there is white space in the diary of my team. They often fill it with amazing innovative things. For example, we use Trello as I'm sure many teams out there do to run projects and collaborate in the workplace, well Morgan who is in my team the other day was telling me that she had used some of her time to create Trello Bots. I had no idea what these were and now I do. They help to automate your tasks to make your work life more efficient. Boom! If we allow space, the innovation will come from within.

Many businesses put innovation as a priority in their corporate strategy and many leaders are asked If them and their team can come up with new ideas, processes

Empower

Remember when I talked about the emotioneering triangle in the introduction. From fear to courage, then confidence.

I remember the early days in my management career I worked with my mentor and line manager Matt Cook at the time. I used to call him many times a day to talk through the situation on the team and the challenges that came up. I wanted to run most things by him. Then one day he left the company for a better opportunity, and I was devasted. 'Who would I phone now?' is what I thought. After a few days of getting over the fact that he had left the company whilst sitting at my desk, I had a eureka moment... He hardly ever told me no. He would ask me what I thought the solution was and what I planned to do about it, would listen to my idea and then encourage me to make it happen. I would leave the call feeling empowered. All that encouragement made me so empowered to take action. Something that I know has contributed to my career success so far.

I recently interviewed Matt Wilson CEO of Einstein Marketer for the Emotioneering podcast, and in the interview, we talked about him learning his craft, then passing it on to his team and trusting them to get better at it. He said one of the most challenging things for him in the start was catching himself when he thought 'I'll just do it because I'm faster'. He knew that he had to give them the opportunity to learn. In his words "they are better than me now at their specific roles".

Hire them then inspire them and hopefully, you won't ever have to fire them.

Self-Awareness

Do you know what your emotional kryptonite is? One of mine is being asked 'what's for dinner tonight?'. Depending on my mood this one phrase can trigger an emotional response in the form of frustration. Although we won't go too much into that in this book today. (Definitely a conversation for after a glass of wine with friends on that one). Think about some of the situations that trigger you in your life, either personal or in the workplace. The thing is we all get them although have you ever wondered why? This is often because of our values being crossed. One of my values is 'Support' and if I ever see someone being unsupported or spoken to in a way that is quite damaging then it can really trigger my reaction and desire to speak up or do something about it. A lot of conflicts can arise in our life when these life values that we hold close to us are crossed. For example, some people value money whilst another person may value generosity. These two values can coexist it's just about understanding them and being aware of our emotions so that we can pause and respond rather than react.

It's all about having self-awareness which is defined as 'the psychological state in which oneself becomes the attention'. Deep work. Study on yourself. Personal development. There are two types of self-awareness, public self-awareness, how others see you and private self-awareness, how you view yourself. The ego, which we all have is very concerned about public self-awareness can throw barriers up when we are given feedback so if you can quieten the ego and listen you really can learn things from others. Although as a wise person once said, 'seek counsel and not opinion', what they meant was to get feedback from someone who knew what they were talking about. Your team are those people that can really help you learn. Your private self-awareness though is even more important and it's how you view yourself. Many people have low self-esteem, and this can affect behaviour, often due to a lack of understanding about themselves. There's a lot of work that can be done to understand your ego, your preferred method of communication or personality type, your values and your emotional intelligence. The benefit of this is absolutely worth the investment of time.

I interviewed Jennifer Louise, Founder of the Successful Salon Club for the Emotioneering Podcast on Ep. 64. Jennifer was extremely open in sharing her journey of discovery as a leader in that she asked her team for their anonymous feedback and told them to hold back on nothing. She says it was an emotional process all those years ago although one of the things she thought she was quite good at was communication although when she asked the team for feedback she found that the team said this was one of the worst areas. Jennifer of course has worked on this, got her Obsessions Salon to a level of operational excellence, and now helps others to do the same. We don't know what we don't know.

How we see ourselves vs how others see us is an evolving process.

Canaries Only Sing In Great Environments

When a person chooses to start a business and becomes a leader, they might have never led a team of people before. The alternative is that they did lead a team although weren't given feedback on their leadership style or worked with leaders that focused only on discipline and accountability as a method of improvement. So then that was the style they learned.

Within an organisation, many people are promoted into leadership roles because they show leadership qualities already or because they are the best performing salesperson. The second reason is not such a great one and can leave the person quite overwhelmed leading a team of people when they haven't done it before.

Maybe you have identified that you have some development work to do so hired someone else to look after the people for you. Now that person has either started to show great results from bringing their experience in or it's the reverse, they did well in the interview although now that certain scenarios are happening repeatedly you realise that they weren't quite at the level you need them to be.

Many new leaders fail within the first 18 months of a new role. According to our source Leaders Beacon, it is 38% of them.

Only 5% of organisations have implemented leadership development into their strategy. Leaving 95% which is a big opportunity.

Even more staggeringly 79% of employees will quit due to a lack of appreciation from their boss.

Having a modern mindset to lead others is the answer to happy healthier teams. It starts with how important you feel leadership training and development is...

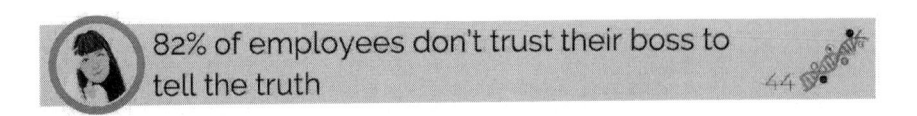

82% of employees don't trust their boss to tell the truth   44%

Emotioneering It

- Ensure leadership training for all people leaders and apply The Canary Concept I created by remembering - Communication, Appreciation, Notice, Acceptance, Relationships, Imagination, Empower, Self-Awareness. C.A.N.A.R.I.E.S (we do run a course on this and I plan a whole book around leadership so watch this space)

- Encourage learning courses in Emotional Intelligence to improve their understanding of themselves and how to communicate effectively and empathetically with their team.

- Run 365-degree feedback initiatives for the leaders to learn about how they come across to others for opportunities to improve.

- Do not stand for rude, unempathetic or uncaring people leaders. If people leave because of them, cry because of them or are scared of them these are all extremely loud alarm bells. It's time for a change.

- Ensure you spend time with your leaders and run goal setting and coaching sessions with them regardless of what level in the business. All people benefit from support and guidance when it is with the right person.

- The ability to speak in public and present to teams is a requirement and public speaking is something that many people are fearful of. Provide training and support in this area.

- Do they have the relationships AND the results? Both are required for a team to win. Do not settle for less.

• ♥ • ♥ • ♥ • ♥ • ♥ •

Six

Execution

♥

It's In The Doing Not The Talking

There will have been some key moments in this book where you have thought "Ah-ha! That's what we need to do!" and I hope so as it is the very reason, I wrote this book to help uncover the opportunities for you in reaching full potential. The thing is unless you actually put any of it into practice then there will be no change. A wise human once told me "If you implement the plan you cannot fail!" and leading on from that, if you do not implement the plan then you truly will.

The Result = Your Ability to Execute at All Costs

The speed at which you can make the changes will also be a contributing factor although it is a balancing act. Act too quickly risk the lack of buy-in to your ideas and the process, act too slowly risk losing momentum, staff and having to start over before seeing the results.

Remember this...

$$\text{The Emotioneering Business Formula is} -$$

$$(P+E+A+C) \times E = \text{Record Breaking Team Results}$$

$$\text{i.e. (People + Engagement + Activities + Culture)} \times \text{Execution)}$$

And **P.E.A.C.E** of mind is certainly one of the benefits that you will get when all of this is implemented.

Challenge your own behaviour and that of others. There will be people that will say to you "but it's always been this way!" or "That won't work because of X Y Z". Don't settle for mediocre or what has always been.

There was once a government leader in central Mexico that had one of the worst affected areas, with people scared to go out at night due to anti-social and violent behaviour. There was no sense of community and it had one of the highest crime rates anywhere had seen. He developed a project because he believed if they painted the building it would make a big difference. Not just in white or a fresh lick of paint. They decided to paint the buildings all bright colours that represented the inside of a skittles packet. Blues, orange, green, red etc. At first, many people thought he was crazy. Over the next few months, everything started to change. People started to stay out longer with their families in the daytime and night-time, there was less rubbish on the streets as everyone felt like they had a home to keep clean and the crime rate fell dramatically. The community really pulled together and the whole atmosphere changed.

Making a massive impact on the overall wellbeing of his people and the happiness in their lives. Not everyone will understand when you start to make changes although they will appreciate the difference and impact it will have on their life when they experience the outcome.

Belief

♥

Do you think it is possible to climb 14 of the largest mountain peaks globally in 6 months? Well, that is exactly what Nim did. 14 Peaks is an incredible achievement story about a man who served in the British military for over 16 years. A Gurkha for 6 years and special forces for over 10 years, Nim Purja MBE started and completed 'Project Possible'. He was doing it for others, to believe in more and to believe that anything in life is possible. He smashed the world record in 6 months and 6 days. The previous record was 8 years. He also holds another 6-speed climbing records which are -

- Most 8000m mountains in the spring season, climbing 6
- Most 8000m mountains in the summer season, climbing 5
- The fastest summit of the 3 highest mountains in the world, Everest, K2, and Kanchenjunga,
- The Fastest summit of the 5 highest mountains in the world, Everest, K2, Kanchenjunga, Lhotse and Makalu
- Fastest lower 8000ers: Gasherbrum 1,2 and Broad Peak
- Fastest higher 8000ers: consecutive summits of Everest, Lhotse and Makalu in 48 hours (Beats his own previous record of 5 days)

Source: Thrudark.com, News, Nims Purja: Beyond Possible: One Soldier, Fourteen Peaks

The thing is, to achieve incredible accolades and have record-breaking results it takes a lot of belief to fuel your execution.

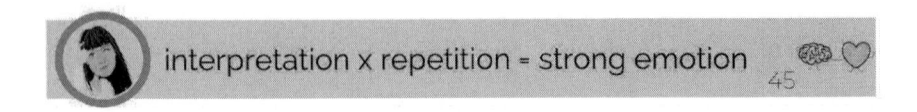

> interpretation x repetition = strong emotion 45

Feed The Faith

Negative thoughts that creep into the mind and start to chip away at our beliefs happen to some of the most well-composed and confident people you know. It happens to almost all of us even if we are not all aware of it.

The challenge can be to spot these thoughts and know your optimism is taking a dip to then take action to build it back up and feed the belief. "Starve the fear and feed the faith" as John C Maxwell says. Miracles and amazing things happen every day. Due to media and our own negative bias, we often don't focus on the good things. This can really take you on a downward spiral.

It's hard to pick yourself back up every day, especially as a business leader that has never done many of the things I talk about in this book before. That takes determination and courage. I can only speak with confidence because I have implemented and influenced all of the elements, I talk about in this book then seen the success that it can bring. The question is, what are you going to do to feed your faith and belief that it will work?

Remove The Roadblocks

♥

"Melissa, you really astonish me sometimes with your resilience, no matter what comes up you always find another way. You are not a jumping flea and always stay that way" said Paul, who recruited me as a Performance Consultant and had seen me grow through the company after a late-night call about the account I was currently working on. With no explanation, he told me to go and look it up. Here is the story I found and exactly what he meant –

The students sat in the lecture hall and were intrigued by the three jars that sat on the table. When the university professor came into the hall, he hurriedly asked the students what would happen if he tipped the collection of live fleas, he was carrying into the first jar. "They will jump out" shouted one of the students. Right! He tipped them into the jar and indeed they jumped out. He asked them again although told them this time he would leave a lid on for 30 seconds, then asked "now what do you think will happen?", most of the students believed they would still jump out. So, he proceeded to tip them into the jar. Most of the fleas escaped although some of them continued to only jump to where the lid was repeatedly. Interesting. He ran the experiment for the last time, this time he would leave the lid on for 60 seconds, "Now what will happen he asked", the students agreed that some would jump out and some would stay. The professor tipped them in for a final time and waited 60 seconds. When he removed the lid, astonishingly NONE of the fleas escaped. They continued to jump to where the lid was. The moral of the story the Professor proclaimed was this, "Life is going to throw challenges in your way, time and time again, roadblocks where you feel there is no way out, remember not to put a lid on your own life, do not be a jumping flea.

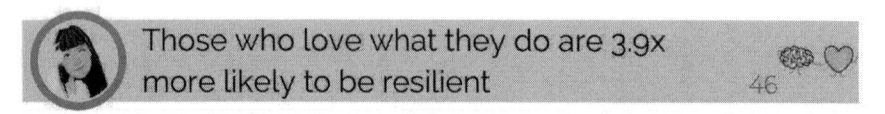

> Those who love what they do are 3.9x more likely to be resilient 46

Don't Put The Limits On Yourself

There are going to be many roadblocks in your way. Some people around you don't believe what you believe. Processes and policies that have been there that are almost set in stone, now have to change. Overcoming your own thoughts about what others will think when you start to expect and drive many new initiatives will be a big challenge. Underestimating the time management and prioritising that it will take to ensure full implementation of the blueprint is another roadblock. The fact that there are so many distractions, number one being you and your own habits, take your mobile phone as an example, will come up and need to be overcome. Can you get out of your own way? Do you want to talk to your team about making changes although want to pick the 'right time'?. Your beliefs have been created as part of your experiences up until this point as well as everyone else's. All of these considerations are valid before we even come on to talking about making the initiatives a reality by taking action and getting it done. You will also come up against roadblocks such as 'will this work in our sector or vertical?'. The key is in asking 'how can we make this work for us?' rather than will it or won't it.

•♥•♥•♥•♥•♥•

Ownership

♥

Since losing my dad and working away a lot I had piled on the pounds, flights, long drives, inconvenient times, and I was reaching for often very unhealthy options. I remember being on the phone with my mum and yet another long drive home and complaining about how I felt about it. For goodness' sake I used to be a personal trainer and fit as a fiddle, now look at me, I thought. My mum, bless her heart said, "It's totally understandable, you are working away, driving long hours and stopping at services so the only options are for you to eat junk etc so don't blame yourself" WOW now my mum was making excuses for me too. No, no, no, no, no! I was making a CHOICE. There were many other people doing similar work to me that didn't put on weight. In this story, I was making an excuse and now others were making them for me too. We have a choice. There is a world of choice for many of us. The next time I was on a trip I really could stop and ask myself, "Which one is it going to be this time, Melissa? The supermarket for a salad or a fast-food restaurant for junk?".

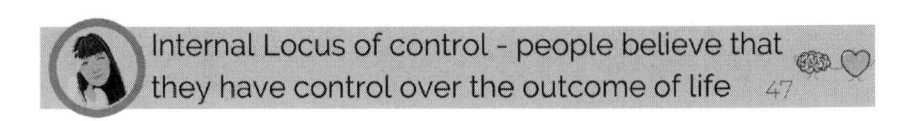

> Internal Locus of control - people believe that they have control over the outcome of life   47

Are You Playing The Blame Game?

Ask yourself am I playing the excuse and blame game or am I willing to take total responsibility. Because with total responsibility comes ownership and with ownership, the magic can truly begin.

Taking total responsibility for what is happening as I mentioned earlier is hard because many people become attached to the ideal scenario or the outcome when in reality it is the day-to-day process, initiatives and habits that lead to the outcome. When you implement the plan, you cannot fail. No one can promise you 'the result' but you will get 'a result' much further towards your goal than you expected when you focus on what it takes to get there. That being said, what I have often seen in my experience is that this framework implemented well has brought results beyond what any leader often thought possible. Are you pointing the finger at others? Or are you leading from the front showing what is possible? It's one thing to direct action, it's another thing to demonstrate it and be there when the magic is being made.

Often, we can pray for a better day or say things like 'when I get this then I will be able to...'. Start now it's not about the tools you have, it's about being resourceful and practical with what you do have. No one is coming to save you and the world owes you nothing. Like the sign on my desk says that I am looking at while writing this, 'make it happen!'.

Find The Who For You

♥

I've been on quite a few prospect calls with potential customers and there is nothing better than when the person you have started to build a relationship with from the start, then starts to sell your services in front of you, to the other decision-makers. These are your advocates, your champions. The people that absolutely get what you do and will bring others along for the journey.

If a stranger ran up to you on the street and said "Don't go to that restaurant, I didn't feel so good after there last week". You would probably think "weirdo" and still go in without much hesitation. However, imagine if you bumped into Leanne, your friend you've known for years and she said exactly the same thing, you would be halfway across the street choosing a different restaurant before she could finish the sentence.

We need a bit of help from the people that care about all this almost as much as we do. Nothing great was ever created alone. If you want to go fast go alone if you want to go far go together.

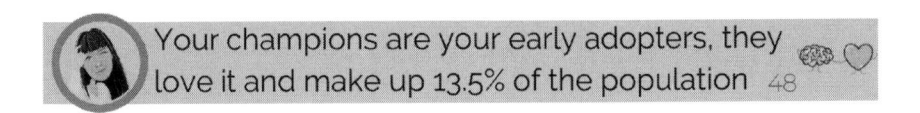

> Your champions are your early adopters, they love it and make up 13.5% of the population 48

Champions & Integrators

A business leader is often a generalist and can't be expected to do it all to an exceptional level. We talked about vision in the last section. Whilst a business owner can be a visionary and an integrator there comes a point where many leaders appoint an integrator. For example, a CEO hires a COO. The CEO may be the person that is close to the vision and the why. The COO understands and is passionate about the vision and the why although stay close to the 'how'. Driving action forward and looking at the strategy in detail much more closely.

The challenge can also arise in pinpointing who is the right fit for a champion or integrator. Champions and integrators can sit at different levels of the company. They must share their passion and be able to demonstrate best practices. Over the years I have seen champions appointed only to not be the right person. Leaders can end up choosing a person because they like them or believe in them more than that person actually believes in the framework or strategy. If they do not embody the best behaviours, then they are not the right person to help you drive this forward. Ask yourself do they over exceed and are highly engaged? Do they speak to the same internal cultural language and are just as passionate about people leadership and team performance?

Training Not A Magic Pill

♥

One of the biggest things to happen in the last few years was the rise of Chess and the Queen's Gambit written by Walter Tevis, which appeared on Netflix as one of the hottest series releases in the last decade. The purchase of chess boards went through the roof and the popularity of the game has increased massively. In chess, the great players are called Grandmasters. They use strategies and predict the next moves through the memory of the patterns of play. These are learned over years and years of playing. My husband, Steve is also a keen player since watching the show and has racked up thousands of hours online playing against people all over the world. Over 4000 games played to date. There isn't a week that goes by that he doesn't watch strategy videos on YouTube to improve and learn. My childhood was also spent taking my brother, Julian to many chess championships as part of the school chess club. Chess is all about learning, memory and strategy.

Chess was also one of the first games to be tackled in the AI world. In fact, the great Kasparov was studied, and his moves were put into electronic boards that would be bought by fans. Yes! My brother had one of these as well as his friends. So why am I taking you on this trip down 'memory lane'? (I love a good cheesy pun). Well in 1973 Chase and Simon studied the Grandmasters against computers and wanted to know the outcome of the grandmasters based on randomised board setups and actual games they or other grandmasters had played. What they found was that the grandmasters only accurately could predict the next moves when the board set up was not randomised. Concluding that learning must have meaning. This is ground-breaking because what had been believed before about learning styles was thrown into question. Whether visual, kinesthetic or auditory as styles, the overall consensus is that *'learning must have meaning'*. There is a great TED talk by Tesia Marshik on learning styles that I recommend checking out.

Another of the great things to know about learning is The Ebbinghaus Forgetting Curve. Herrmann Ebbinghaus ran a study on learning and memory over periods of time. He plotted the memory on a graph and created the concept of the 'Strength of Memory'. The Ebbinghaus forgetting curve shows how information is lost over time when there is no attempt to retain it. Meaning that seeds are planted in the training room, how they are cultivated, and how the knowledge is retained is all in what happens afterwards. So training is not a magic pill that will fix all. It's a necessary starting point that sets the expectations and foundations of the learning. Complete learning is about transformation change, retained knowledge and practical application of the theory.

> We only remember 50% of what we hear within in the first hour then 25% in the 2nd

Retraining & Retaining The Knowledge

"We've sent him on the training six times now and he still doesn't seem to pick it up...". This is a common instance in the workplace where just because we have sent them on the training then they 'should' be able to deliver. This is not the case. It also depends on the competence of the trainers and the way they facilitate the topic.

I've also seen far too many times training being used as a tick box exercise like the example of wellbeing initiatives being seen as projects. Bringing an outsourced company in to deliver some training on mental health and then never really following it up for long term benefits. Change requires practical implementation of the learning and for this to be assessed then coached to. Earlier in the book, I talked about one to one sessions having a greater impact. This is the truth as the classroom training plants the seeds, helps them understand the coaching and when followed by support from leaders to implement the knowledge this is when behaviour change takes place. As mentioned above the learning 'must have meaning' so bringing it in line with their goals and real-life examples will encourage the changes to take place.

I'm all for training and have delivered over 1000 in-person workshops in my career, what is often in my mind is what will happen after the training is delivered and the person goes back to their workplace. Also, the challenge can be that the person on the course may have had no-decision in the process to attend the training. When I think of all the times, I have learned the best it was when I really wanted to be there.

There is also something to be said for repeat training as a refresher within a certain time frame. If we know that we will only retain 25% of a workshop, then repeating the process does have benefits at increasing knowledge retention and competence when it is supported. Although if there is no willingness to change or learn then it won't be worth it.

Excellence Is Not Convenient

♥

In Wales UK there is a little town called Cowbridge. In that town, there is one of the longest standing award-winning vineyards in Wales, The Glyndwr Vinyard. It was my friend's birthday, so we arranged a vineyard tour and lunch. This stunning location was right on our doorstep, and we never even knew it was there. The last few years since 2020 have really helped us to be grateful for our local surroundings. Whilst we were on the tour this very enthusiastic son of the owner was showing us around and for many years, I had not really stopped to think about what goes into making wine apart from those videos you see posted on YouTube of people in big wooden tubs stomping barefoot on the grapes.

This young winemaker was telling us about every single thing that goes into making this liquid that many of us drink, the weather being an extremely big factor, the budding of the vines and having to light fires at the crack of dawn on the days that there might be a late frost, not to ruin their season through lost produce. The whole process is certainly not convenient and makes a massive difference to the end results. That consistency, the obsession about the weather, the hard work and graft that went into each season is key to their success.

I am nowhere near calling myself a vineyard expert although I know one thing, people buy their wine for this reason. The due care and attention that goes into creating every drop. I certainly made sure to purchase a few bottles and they tasted so much better knowing what had gone into making them.

The point is, do you think it was convenient for Michael Phelps the American Olympic Swimmer, when he used to get up at 4, am to hit the pool at 5 am?

No!

Do you think it was convenient for Nim Purja to drag himself and his team one step at a time up and down 14 peaks over 6 months?

No!

Do you think it was convenient for Gary Vaynerchuck CEO of Vayner Media and builder of Wine Library to drive 6 hours to a woman's house just before the holidays when they made a mistake?

No!

I once had the opportunity to be in a room with Les Brown one of the all-time greatest speakers and here's what he said: "If you do everything that's easy your life is going to be hard; if you do everything that's hard, your life is going to be easy".

Put the effort in now and the results that follow will be worth it.

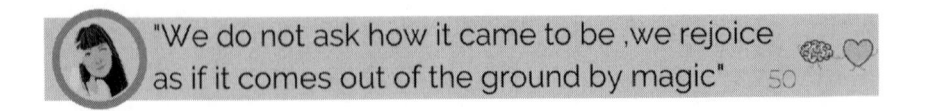

> "We do not ask how it came to be, we rejoice as if it comes out of the ground by magic" 50

Convenience Comes At A Price

In the workplace, corners get cut a lot of the time. It's in our nature as human beings and mammals to reserve time and energy although not great when you want something done well or you are driving towards excellence. Convenience comes at a hefty price and I'm not just talking about a jar of coffee from your local corner shop. If leaders choose what is easy over what is the right way for things to be done, you will see blunt words being spoken with no diplomacy, you will see poor performance in underskilled staff because it's easier to not train them, you will see employees not following the process with customers leading to poor service and lack of retention as well as many more. Can you notice when this is being done or when you are doing it yourself?

A whole world has been created through convenience right at our fingertips. Through technology. You will see employees and leaders send emails rather than calling people for a conversation. Of course, some communication is fine by email, what's app, text is fine although choosing it completely over face-to-face interaction and relationship building is not, especially for difficult feedback that must be given. Written text does not have tone or inflexion behind it, so it is very open to interpretation. Face to face communication is better to see the congruence and manner that it was intended.

Also, miscommunication or lack of understanding can occur.

TLDR - Which for those that are not down with the cool kids, stands for 'Too Long Didn't Read'. Are they even reading the emails or the messages when you send them?

Actions & Follow Up

♥

Elvis probably said it best for this chapter, in one of his greatest songs, "A little less conversation, a little more action please" There's a time for being, a time for thinking, a time for talking and a time for doing! Like this section about execution covers, there is value in explanation and influence although once there is agreement it's time to do something about it. Only after the action is taken and all is implemented can we then assess the effectiveness or the new potential available.

Quite often over the years, I have attended business meetings with teams. Month after month, the same things would come up consistently. The situation was that there would often be no minutes sent over following the meeting, and there would be no follow up on any actions agreed to the following month. I soon suggested that the front slide of the meeting be changed to address the actions from the last month first, before moving on to the performance impact. This very soon started to move the needle. Far too many meetings with actions and goals taken away are with no date to be done by as well as no name next to them for who is responsible. And it's not about doing everything all at once it's about implementing the blueprint on a priority basis from the foundations then having the focus to keep adding more actions until all are covered.

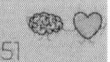

> A person earning 40k will waste 15k a year procrastinating for 3 hours a day 51

Avoidance of Commitment

I talked about responsibility earlier. When it comes to actions and follow up, our emotional brain will often want us to shy away from the pressure of committing to something. Whether that is a revenue number or making sure we complete a project. Think about how many plans are made and discussed in the workplace and then fall by the wayside. Regardless of whether it is a frontline employee or a leader within an organisation, this can affect us all. Often commitment is avoided by those that are more scared of failure. They will see not getting to where they want to be as a big setback, on the flip side there are team members that are much more comfortable with failing and may over commit.

Regardless of whether someone is avoiding commitment or overestimating what they can achieve it's about finding balance and encouraging people to fail fast learn quickly. Many people prefer to work with someone that believes they can achieve anything. They might miss the mark a few times although often they will achieve way more than the average. Supporting a person to get to this point and overcome their tendency to avoid commitment though is extremely rewarding. It's all about their journey through small steps and reassurance that you believe in them. Often way more than they believe in themselves.

All actions and follow up lead to positive stress in the long run which actually affects our wellbeing for the good because we get a sense of achievement and the dopamine rush.

Accountability

♥

We talked about accountability a little earlier in terms of a leader holding employees to account. This part is about you holding other leaders to account for executing the blueprint, results and relationships. Let me ask you this...

What is the difference between a tadpole, a baby chick and a human baby? The tadpole bursts its way out of the frogspawn, the baby chick hatches its way out of a shell and a human baby? Well, we are pushed and nurtured into this world. Like most mammals.

That's right! We don't crawl out of a pond or peck our way out of anything, we are PUSHED into this world. It's part of our nature. Now, I'm not saying that we should carry on going around pushing people about. What I am saying is that it's very interesting to me when I look at the facts this way and line them up against the biggest results, we see from people that it is often mostly when they have had a coach or a mentor.

Someone that is encouraging and supportive, yet the bottom line is that they also hold you accountable to do the things you said you were going to do.

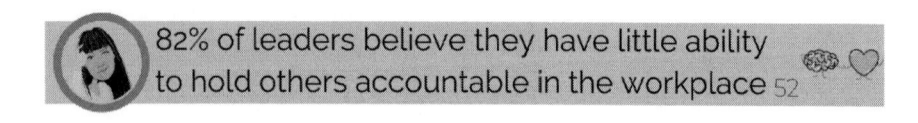

> 82% of leaders believe they have little ability to hold others accountable in the workplace [52]

Candour & Consequence

With your team, it's about ensuring that there are consequences for things that aren't done or consistent low performance. The emotioneering side of things is that all of us are motivated by what we don't want far more than what we are moving towards. The challenge can be that there is far too much accountability or there has not been enough opportunity to get things right. This is a fearsome organisation. The fearless organisation is where there is a balance from a supportive, encouraging, and accountable workplace.

Without accountability, your best people won't stay or your customers and unfortunately your poor performers will. The challenge can also be to make accountability fair. If you have two people do the same thing through gross misconduct and one gets to stay because of their sales performance and the other one must go, then this is going to send out a very bad signal to other employees.

There can be a lack of understanding from leadership on what to say or how to approach something or how to follow disciplinary procedures in many cases leaving it down to HR to lead. This means the person with the best relationship isn't the one giving the feedback which can feel even worse. Many small businesses won't have a HR department or people manager so the emotional impact on whether they are doing it right or saying the right thing can cause stress and anxiety.

The Narrative To The Numbers

♥

One of the biggest misconceptions of the world today is this - "The population is just increasing and increasing".

Not that there is really any sort of limit that has ever been set on the planet, still this is something that many think and many say. Okay, I know the planet has limited resources. (Elon Musk and team, work harder on the Mars dream please). Now it is currently increasing although it isn't 'just' increasing. That is part of the misconception. We usually assume when looking at data that lines will 'just' continue to go straight when that 'just' is not the case.

Hans Rosling released one of my favourite books called Factfullness. In there he tells of the time he took the UN population graph to a teachers' conference and asked them to choose the exact amount that the UN predicted for the population of children between 0 – 15 by the year 2100.

A)   4 billion (over double the amount in 2000)

B)   3 billion (over 50% increase than in 2000) or

C)   2 billion (a slight increase to 2050 then no further increase i.e. No new children)

He told them one was real and the other two were made up.

Without reading ahead what do you think the answer is?

The UN experts expect by 2100 that the number of children will not increase. The answer is C.

As humans, we have an inner instinct that protects us to dodge a hit in the face, predict the positioning of cars around us on the motorway or hit the ball in tennis. So, it's only natural that we predict the next course of events based on the current situation. So, massive spikes in performance seem unlikely as well as massive downturns in performance. They are possible though.

As a performance consultant, it's why I use the Emotioneering Business Blueprint to assess opportunities with performance through areas of improvement. It's important that we positively challenge the status quo and inspect what we expect. When doing strategy calls and discoveries they bring about so much understanding and value.

Remember "people make numbers, numbers don't make people"

Years ago, I was sitting at a board meeting with a retail client and one of the business analysts announced, only 'X' amount of our customers take more than one premium product with us. I pondered on this, of course, it was across the whole of the network although based on my time in the field working with the most operationally excellent teams, I knew this was what the data was saying however the narrative behind the numbers was quite different. Looking at numbers in isolation like this in business means that someone could say "oh well let's only offer one product to them then instead of more" which could be catastrophic to the whole business or quite the opposite if it was a high number when then the question could be if the products were being offered correctly.

When you then take an emotioneering approach to this it's important to understand the behaviour of people, because on analysis imagine 80

– 90% of the salespeople had a "yes" on one product they then decided (through fear of rejection or losing the whole sale) not to offer another even though it would benefit the customer. The data for 10 – 20% of the locations in the network that had better operations and leadership teams was that 15x more customers purchased multiple products. What a difference. The question can be "How do we enable all of the lower performing locations to deliver what the 10 -20% of operationally excellent locations do? NOT "Should we actually care about offering a second product at all?"

Know your numbers. Dig deeper. The devil is in the detail, and retail is detail

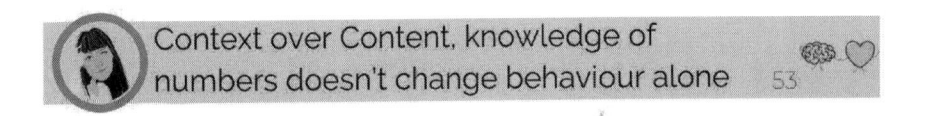

> Context over Content, knowledge of numbers doesn't change behaviour alone 53

The Devil is in The Detail

When you cannot talk to the numbers, or you don't know the story behind them in the workplace during presentations and when sharing them, you lose the ability to help people connect with what you are trying to convey. For example, if I tell you that our average sales conversion for the year is 12% it would mean nothing. How are you to know if that is good or bad? It has no context.

If I, then told you that this was the average and that the top 25% of team members were above 35% sales conversion then your mind would start to question why the average was much lower and who the people were that were below 12%. What if I then went on to tell you that when we started looking at the performance the average conversion was only 5% which was 3 months ago. Then it would provide a reason to feel good that it was going in the right direction.

Presenting numbers and no narrative can really lose your credibility, belief in the process as well as boring your audience to tears.

Imagine saying something like 50% of our customers surveyed love the packaging. It could also be quite deceiving when there were only 2 survey responses.

♥ ♥ ♥ ♥ ♥

Inspiring Action

♥

When you work in the world of human and business development it might sound cliché but every day, we really do have the ability to change people's lives.

I once had the opportunity to ask Les Brown, one of the greatest motivational speakers of our time, a question about what he says to himself before he got up to do a motivational talk to audiences around the world. I had always had a phrase I said to myself before going into a training room, presentation or speaking opportunity so I wondered what Les Brown said to himself. He answered, "Less of me, more of thee". I loved it! He always goes in with the audience in mind and what they needed to get from him today.

Have a think about the people that inspire action in you. Those moments you won't forget from amazing people. Ask yourself what made them inspirational? Their energy, their clarity, their passion.

I also met Tim Story, life coach to the stars, organised by the Winners Club, and asked him to write a quote for me on a piece of card and sign it. He wrote 'You are believable!' what he meant was that the way I speak and the way I share the message helps others believe in it too. Not 'unbelievable'. Being believable means that you help others believe that little bit more so that they take steps and action to change their own lives. How believable are you?

> Inspired employees will produce 21% more profitability overall
> 54

A Barrier to Learning & Behaviour Change

33% of people say that uninspiring content is a barrier to learning. Based on Tesia Marshik's TED talk about learning, what we know is that it must have meaning. When we fail to make our conversations or training relatable that is something that will be a barrier to inspiring action. The leader often only knows what they know and without knowing what their people are about they will struggle to inspire them. Neuro-Linguistic Practitioners will also call it a pattern interrupt, something unexpected to pique interest to keep the audience engaged.

It could also be the poor public speaking or storytelling ability of a leader that could hinder this. When speaking to many leaders over my career they have stories, many of them much like the ones I have shared with you in this book although because they have never paused to reflect, see their relevance or how it could impact their employees, they are never told.

Employees are influenced and inspired by many people on a day-to-day basis, whether it is on their social media via Tik-Tok or a motivational talk on YouTube, or by strong role models in their life, they have access to inspiration every day. The challenge is because of this stimulus, the comparison to a traditional and uninspiring leader can cause them to be demotivated and lose focus. Look at the physical environment and assess whether it is inspirational, does it bring the team together? Is there a team board or a collective space for communication? Is it dull and lacking vibrancy?

Seven

Conclusion

So, there you have it. A collection of initiatives to be able to emotioneer business results with my Emotioneering Business Blueprint.

Whether that is profits, professionally developed people or world-class engagement, you now have the ingredients to lead a team that can achieve record-breaking results through high performance.

Now you might be thinking that I haven't gone heavy on the service and sales process within this book. Now of course I am a great salesperson, sales coach and trainer, although I am sure you have your processes for that and you have been making sales through service long before you picked up this book. The first place to start is in the analysis of the current performance and then by implementing everything that I have talked about in here to support your service and sales, the results will no doubt go through the roof.

I can tell you that when the Emotioneering Business Blueprint is implemented you will see those results you crave and even better it will unlock the potential you have been looking for.

The Emotioneering Business Blueprint is a people operations and performance strategy.

So, yes! It is possible to do.

Although you now have a decision to make. Ask yourself these questions -

1) Can I do this myself?

2) Do I need support with this?

3) Can someone do this for me?

We absolutely can help you -

<u>Get Your Free Emotioneering Business Scorecard</u>

We have a way of doing this for you because we've been doing it for years. It's the Emotioneering Business Scorecard that will ask you a series of questions and be able to give you a score against the 13 key areas of focus within the Emotioneering Business Blueprint. This will give you much more clarity and understanding of what to do first, creating an impact and start moving towards implementing the whole blueprint.

I'm offering you as a reader of this book a free performance strategy call with our team to provide you with this analysis and talk you through it with our expertise. Make our day and let us do what we love by helping businesses and teams succeed. Email info@modernmindgroup.co.uk today to arrange your call and get your scorecard today!

3 Levels of Support Services

We have a different level of support depending on where you are in your business to drive the implementation of The Emotioneering Business Blueprint

Level 1. Elevate - Done Yourself With Support
Level 2. Collaborate - Done With You
Level 3. Accelerate - Done For You and With You

Using a blend of consultancy, courses, training and coaching to suit your needs following analysis of the Emotioneering Business Score on a monthly basis.

Training & Courses

Having delivered over 1000 in-person workshops I love to deliver classroom training or virtual training to teams. We also offer e-learning courses. We can create them for you or deliver our courses which have had great feedback.

We offer training for -

Leadership

Emotional Intelligence

Communication / Soft Skills

Emotioneering Business Results

Service & Sales

Mental Health Awareness

Mental Health Champion

The Emotioneering Podcast

Check out the Emotioneering Podcast to hear the discussions and learning points on this book. It is available on Apple, Spotify, Podbean or Google.

The Newsletter

Get our free monthly newsletter by subscribing on the website -

Modern Mind Group

www.modernmindgroup.co.uk

We are Emotioneering Human Performance, Not Engineering it! Because We Are Driven By Emotion.

Here Are Some Testimonials of What Our Clients say -

As a unique ability, your positivity comes to mind and you give 100% or 120% at times. It was good for us that you were not just a theorist, but you were practical and experienced in taking action, you worked in sales teams, you came from the ground up, from a salesperson to sales manager but then through that devolved into a performance consultant for working with teams. So, that's valuable. Your eagerness, and willingness not just to make your consultancy fee (I feel like it's worth every penny by the way) but also to show that you want to make a change and you genuinely care about the people you work with. There is a real sincerity in working with you - Alisa CEO - AZ Real Estate

"Your consulting style made it easy for our clients to completely trust you and you developed a way of allowing ambitious goals to be seen as achievable. Instrumental in transformational long term changes for our clients, who still talk about what was achieved" Paul - Vice President of EMEA

Melissa is genuine and authentic and spending time around Melissa is great for your soul. Melissa's work ethic is incredible. She is a problem solver, a genius and a solution finder. If Melissa offers you a set of results - I assure you that you will get more than that. - Danielle - Business Consultant

It was an absolute pleasure to have Melissa as our consultant for the internal team performance excellence project! She did a fantastic job and has introduced some disruptive and challenging advances in our work. The insights from her work are impressive and have a real impact. As a manager, I am very thankful for Melissa's valuable advice and for her encouragement to go out of my comfort zone. That's where personal development and team success lie! - Anna Operations Director - AZ Real Estate

Melissa is someone who truly embodies how to engage teams and individuals, both internally and externally. She has been successful in improving engagement and implementing cultural changes with clients. Melissa has proven herself over the years in terms of training and content creation that delivers results and makes a lasting impact. Her presentation style is captivating as her passion for training and coaching is clear from the outset. Melissa displays strong interpersonal skills and a unique capacity for empathy, which is why she has the ability to motivate those around her. Being a critical thinker, with strong emotional intelligence, Melissa is someone I would highly recommend to business owners looking to take their culture, employees and performance to the next level. - Mark - Talent Development Director

"The biggest takeaway for me from your Mental Health Awareness Course was definitely how to help support people who are struggling. It can sometimes be easy to spot the signs or have someone even tell you what they are going through or how they are feeling, but hard to know how to deal with it or help the person feel supported, so I have taken away techniques to break down how best to support someone" - John General Manager at Virgin Active

One of the best listeners I've come across and you've inspired me. It feels personal. You actually care. I think the aura that you give off is infectious and positivity, breeds, positivity. It's definitely changed my life in sales and in my personal life so far. It's life-changing 100%. Your coaching has brought more revenue to the business and more commission for us, we've certainly increased sales and revenue. And that's all down to the fact that they've begun to trust me a lot more now because I've got more self-belief. It's not just that you're going to gain a coach. You'll gain a friend, somebody that you can really trust. Coaching with Melissa changes your whole aspect of life itself, anybody would be very lucky to have you - Sharon Sosa - Airport Manager - Car Rental

Final Word

I hope that I can now call you an Emotioneer and you have bought into the emotioneering way. I really wish you all the success with the development of your team and would love to hear the feedback on this book and what has happened since you implemented what I have told you. Feel free to give us a tag on social media, you can find the company and myself on all platforms.

Let's emotioneer those business results!

Best wishes

Melissa Curran

Acknowledgments

Thank You From The Bottom of My Heart

Firstly thank you to you for reading this all the way to this point. I appreciate every person that has purchased a copy of this book to support the cause. I really wish you well in your journey of Emotioneering. You are now an Emotioneer!

Stephen, my husband, you are my rock and thank you for supporting me endlessly. From the day we met until now you have had my back and I have had yours. I love you. This is for our future.

Thanks be to God. I am blessed and grateful.

My Team & Inner Circle

Nothing great was ever created without a team...

Morgan Clements, thank you firstly for the book art and your creativity to illustrate the concepts of the chapters. Secondly, without you supporting all of the social media and content, from writing articles, the newsletter and scheduling all the posts, this book would not have been a reality at this point. I wish you every success in your future and I am so happy to have been able to help you start your professional career.

Zineb Layachi, the North Star. What can I say?! I class you as on my team and inner circle. Since we met you have been a driving force for the ideas and creativity to come to life. We create, we innovate, we laugh. Thank you for all of your help.

Sensei, Taran Hughes, you have been mentoring me through this process and you must be so relieved the book is finally released. Ha! From the moment you offered to help me by giving feedback on the Mindset score a few years ago I was so grateful to meet you. Your mentorship has meant the world to me. Thank you so much for supporting me with my business development. I am blessed to have had you on the journey.

Clients

To all my clients, new and old. Thank you all for putting your faith in me and the company. You have given me the ability to do what I love to do. It is my passion to emotioneer a better future for you and your teams. The best is yet to come. I look forward to building the future with you. (A special thank you to Alisa, you gave me the rocket fuel to start this book)

Family

To Sonia, my mother. Thank you mam for all the encouragement you have always given me through the years. Showing me how to express myself and the commitment of deliberate practice. My continuous learning and curiosity I owe to you.

To Hugh, my dad, I miss you every day and I would not be doing the work I do today without your engineering mindset being passed on to me. Thank you for all the lessons in my life. I hope we meet again one day and we can sing Hey Jude forevermore.

Julian, AKA the paddleboarding king of wales, congrats on everything you have been building brother. Thank you for the relentless encouragement. I am so proud of you and I know Dad would be too. I'm looking forward to seeing how everything grows over the next few years. I will also be eternally grateful to have had you to grow up with. So many fun memories.

Ali, my sister, we laugh and we cry, then we laugh some more. You have always brought sunshine to my life with your energy and enthusiasm. You were a great role model to me growing up and we got through many tough times together. Ps. You're my favourite sister mind! ;)

Rob, I am extremely proud of the work you do to help those youngsters that need it every day. They have a great person that believes in them and that is more than many get. Also brother, thanks for the festivals, the guitar playing and the singing.

To Donovan, my brother in law. You've been there for me since I was so young, to always listen and help when you can. I am so grateful. Thank you for loving Ali and bringing your world into ours. You've had it tough the last year and you are the most determined/ strong person I know. I wish you health and happiness.

To Elleshia, Christian, Rhys, and Josie. Having nieces and nephews close in age to me have helped me to stay relatable as well as young. Thank you for being, young determined and supportive of your old auntie here as well as putting up with the singing and dancing ha!

Eileen, you are the best mum in law I could ever wish for. Your positivity and zest for life are infectious. Keep going! I am so grateful for your praise and support.

Nicola, the best sis in law ever. From pizza making to christmas decorations we are always up to something. Thank you for being there and flying the flag for strong ambitious women. Josie is very blessed to have you as a mum.

David, (DJ Frostie Farley) thank you for the laughs over the years. Your sense of humour is fantastic and maybe that is where Josie gets a bit of it from.

Steve and Kim, thank you for your support from afar and for visiting when you can. Keep enjoying life and your travels

The wider family, you have all been part of this journey. So grateful.

Friends

Leanne, Alana, Shereen, Sadie, Julie, Danielle, Rawiri, Charlie, Laura and Emily. Thank you for bringing laughter to my life and keeping me grounded. We have so many good memories. Thank you for all your support and encouragement always.

To old friends, new friends and people I have met on my business journey I am grateful for you. When you share your journey it helps me feed my belief to keep going. Thank you.

Volleyball Team

Wow! What a club we have become. Thank you for lifting me up in training and making me feel like I belong. Melanie, Nikki, Nicola, Olga, Phil, Scott & Bart you have been there from the beginning and I am so grateful to you for your patience and help. To the rest of the current team, Maria, Emma, Joy, Annissa, Priscilla, and Debora, let's get winning more games in the league! I am proud to play with you. Go Swans!

Podcasts & Interviews

Thank you to all my guests so far on the Emotioneering Podcast and Radio Show - Michael Cloonan, Simon Day, Phill Tottman, Steve Philip, Bobbie Evans, Cathryn Anwyl Williams, Ademola Adeyeba, Kesha Williams, Natasha Clark, Paul Rees, Zoe Griffiths, Harry Thomas, Camillie Richardson, Mindy Gibbins-Klein, Andrew Lopez, Alex Chisnall, Kev Orkian, Baiju Solanki, Ife Thomas, Ashley Shipman, Mat Wilson, Mark Drager, Jennifer Louise, Alisa Zotimova, Carol Massay, Sarah Abel, Jan Santos, Charlie Oliver, Lucienne Shakir, Lauren Lepley Caldon, Dr Dunni, Richard Masson and all the guests to come.

To all those that have interviewed me for their podcasts and shows, I am grateful for the opportunity -

Simon Day - Speak With Simon

Amy Rowlinson - Focus On Why

Annette Berry - Intouch Networks

Marcus Cauchi - The Inquisitor Podcast

Abigail Barnes - It's Your Time!

Rhonda Williams - Coffee With Rhonda Show

Mindy Gibbins-Klein - The Thoughtful Leader

Raina Jain - The Happiness Project

Azeem Sahir - EI Cafe

Jan Santos - The Creative Scoop

Satu Ahlman - Saga Performance

My Life & Career Mentors

Thank you to all of the people named below for being the people that have shared lessons and guided me in my career as well as life. You have left a last impression on me, offered me opportunities and taken your own time to help me. For all that, I will be eternally grateful.

Robert Palmer, Rachel Keene, John Quirk, Stephanie Hurlow, Henry Engleheart, Rebecca Bogue, Dan Kelly, Andrew Sandbrook, Ed Lane, Kevin Burnham, Matthew Cook, Richard Brown, Mat Winkler, Ross Marshall, Andrew Harding, Abi Selby, Paul Porter, Paul McLoughlin, Aurelien Dumont, Melanie Hofer, Filipe Olivera, Ken Stellon, Tom Diaz, Ziad Khoury, Geoffrey Toffetti, Padraig O'Connell, Brian Hirten, Phil Smith, Gary Barker, Michael Cloonan, Steve Judge, Lucy Philip, Christopher Ashford and Danny Grimshaw.

> **"Be present in all things and thankful for all things"**
> **- Maya Angelou**

Notes

Here are the notes for the stats that are used in the images throughout the book.

1. 88% rejection if a photo is on a CV but 80% of employers search you on social media - Be Hiring
2. Using core competencies reduces improvement and learning time by 50% - Research on educating graduates by Western Governors University
3. Reasons for losing customers or clients are 70% emotional intelligence related - ihhp
4. 36% of employees believe there is a mismatch between their actual skills and what are needed for their role - OECD
5. Employees stay 41% longer when there is internal hiring opportunities - Netsuite
6. Over 70% of discrimination in the workplace is towards race, nationality and disability. The Balance 2020
7. 27% of companies say that the cost of hiring the wrong person is over 50K – BMS Performace
8. Employee exits cost 16% - 213% of their annual salary – Vantage Circle
9. Only 42% of leaders fire based on attitude and behaviours which contribute to poor performance and conflict

10. The top 25% of connected teams see an increase of 41% in absenteeism and 66% in employee wellness - Gallup
11. 77% of companies focus on employee experience - unknown
12. At least 20% more sales from a highly engaged team – The Circular Board
13. A goal written down with a date, communicated to one other person is 80% more likely to be achieved - Modern Mind Group
14. 44% increase in sales when a strong incentive plan is in place – Incentive Solutions
15. 83% of employees would like to provide more input – Employment Crossing
16. Properties with moderate use of In-Gauge see an average increase of 323% in incremental revenue - Frontline Performance Group
17. 70% of employees would leave for better learning and development – Vantage Circle
18. 4/5 employees believe leadership won't act on their responses – officevibe.com
19. Employees performed 87% higher than those who had not had product training – Marshall Fisher – The Value of Helpful Expertise
20. Mental Health Cost UK Employers 45million Per year - Deloitte
21. 47% of workers received feedback 'a few times or less' from their managers - Gallup
22. Poor data can cost businesses 20%–35% of their operating revenue - Fathom
23. #1 Sign of a good one to one is a safe environment for open and honest communication (employees) – Soapbox.com
24. 15 minutes or less will allow the team to become a strong peer accountable team that is focused on the "WIN – metronomeunited.com
25. 74% of workers prefer a collaborative work culture to one where the manager makes all the decisions – Employment Crossing
26. Learners retain 10% of what they read, 25% of what they hear and 90% of what they teach back or put into practice – National Training Laboratory

27. 89% of customers who switch do so because of poor service – Leadfamily.com
28. Employees 40% more engaged and 38% more discretionary effort with effective coaching - Gartner
29. Only 29% of managers find meetings productive – HR Digest
30. Feelings of employee isolation reduce productivity by 21% - Teambuilding.com
31. A surge of activity always came after the temporal midpoint – Connie Gersick
32. 87% of employees agree gamification makes them more productive - TalentLMS
33. 96% of organisations have factored innovation into their business strategy - Mckinnsey
34. 2.5% of people are innovators - E.M.Rogers 1962
35. Only 4/10 employees know what their company mission is - Gallup
36. 49% of employees don't' know their company values – Libertymind.com
37. 81% of employees on Fortunes 100 Best Companies to work for said it was a fun place to work – Great Place To Work Institute
38. The average adult laughs 17 times per day vs 300 as a child – USPM.com
39. Extremely connected teams demonstrate 21% more profitability – goremotely.com
40. 32% of people have felt lonely in the workplace - Forbes
41. 54% of companies report their customer experience operations are managed in silos - Dimension Data CX Benchmarking Report.
42. 79% of people would decline a job offer due to unethical standards – Vantage Circle
43. Before performance initiatives, it is likely that the business only has 25% high performers - Melissa Curran
44. 82% of employees don't trust their boss to tell the truth - Edelman
45. interpretation x repetition = strong emotion – Master your emotions, Thibaut Meurisse
46. Those who love what they do are 3.9x more likely to be resilient – ADP Research Insitute

47. Locus of control is the degree to which people believe that they, as opposed to external forces, have control over the outcome of events in their lives. - Developed by Julian B. Rotter in 1954

48. Your champions are your early adopters, they love it and makeup 13.5% of the population – EM rogers 1962

49. We only remember 50% of what we hear within the first hour then 25% in the 2nd. – Julian Treasure Listening Research

50. "We do not ask how it came to be, we rejoice as if it comes out of the ground by magic" –wrote Nietzsche, quoted in the book Grit by Angela Duckworth

51. A person earning 40k will waste 15k a year procrastinating for 3 hours a day – The Creatives Hour

52. 82% of leaders believe they have little or no ability to hold others accountable in the workplace – Harvard Business Review

53. Context over Content, knowledge of numbers doesn't change behaviour alone – Forbes.com Bryan Robinson P.H.D.

54. Inspired employees produce 21% more profitability – Harvard Business Review

About The Author

Melissa Curran

Founder of The Modern Mind Group and Bestselling Author of Emotioneering Business Results. Melissa has delivered over 15,000 hours of Coaching and over 1,000 Training Workshops - from frontline employees to board level executives.

A trusted, global people operations and performance consultant, working with high profile organisations, for over 8 years in leadership, communication, employee engagement, operational excellence, and culture transformation. Over 15 years experience in service, sales and performance management spanning across, contact centres, retail, hospitality, events, leisure, media, automotive, property and SAAS verticals. Helping leaders with teams emotioneer record-breaking results.

Melissa is the creator of the Emotioneering Business Blueprint, a people operations and performance strategy that is the answer to increased profits, highly engaged teams and record-breaking results. Melissa is driven to help people emotioneer a modern mindset by increasing emotional intelligence, understanding their emotions as well as others, having the confidence to express themselves effectively and being enabled to do that with or without technology. In today's world the ability to combine emotional intelligence, multi-channel communication and technical ability has never been so crucial to success. With a true passion for people development, this has been Melissa's driving motivation for the last 20 years to make an impact and help unlock potential.

Confident and captivating public speaker for events run by companies such as Dell, Swoop Technologies, JPI Media and Futureheads. Awarded 'Game Changer of The Month' by Creative Talk Magazine.

Featured contributer for Your Business Magazine with James Caan

Host of the **Emotioneering Podcast**

Emotioneering Human Performance Not Engineering it!

Linkedin - http://www.linkedin.com/in/melissa-curran-performance-consultant

Instagram - melissacurran_

Twitter - melissacurran_

Clubhouse - melissacurran_